Map 2

Laos

Thailand

South
Vietnam

Cambodia

Qui Nhon

Nha Trang

Cam Ranh Bay

×FSB1

*Elephant Ear*
*(War Zone C)*    FSB2×

Black Virgin Mtn

Tay Ninh

Bien Hoa

Xuan Loc

Cu Chi

Long
Binh

Saigon

Baria    Nui Dat

Vung Tau

0      50      100 miles

**A**LLIES AND **M**ATES

# Allies & Mates

AN AMERICAN SOLDIER WITH THE
AUSTRALIANS AND NEW ZEALANDERS IN
VIETNAM 1966–67

GORDON L. STEINBROOK

UNIVERSITY OF
NEBRASKA PRESS
LINCOLN AND
LONDON

∞ The paper in this book
meets the minimum
requirements of
American National Standard
for Information Sciences—
Permanence of Paper
for Printed Library Materials,
ANSI Z39.48-1984.

Library of Congress
Cataloging-in-
Publication Data
Steinbrook, Gordon L., 1942–
Allies and mates :
an American soldier with
the Australians and
New Zealanders
in Vietnam, 1966–67 /
by Gordon L. Steinbrook.
    p.   cm.
Includes index.
ISBN 0-8032-4238-7
1. Vietnamese Conflict, 1961–1975
—Personal narratives, American.
2. Vietnamese Conflict, 1961–1975
—Australia.
3. Vietnamese Conflict,
1961–1975—New Zealand.
4. Steinbrook, Gordon L., 1942–
DS559.5.S74   1995
959.704′38—dc20
94-1287
CIP

*to my family*

# CONTENTS

# ILLUSTRATIONS

# ACKNOWLEDGMENTS

First, credit for making this book possible must go to my wife, Frances, and to my parents, Elva and Leo Steinbrook. The letters they saved provided the basic content for this record of war.

I am especially indebted and grateful to Peter Maslowski, professor of history, University of Nebraska–Lincoln: without Pete there also would have been no book. His insistence that my letters and memories had potential as a book, his advice as I wrote drafts, his constant encouragement, and his conviction that someday my manuscript would be published are things for which I am ever beholden.

For their help in typing the manuscript drafts, a heartfelt thank-you to a handful of my former high-school history students. Without the efforts of Sarah, Karen, Joyce, Kelly, Linda, Sherry, Lois, and Melody, the whole project could never have gotten under way.

My thanks also to Lana Danielson, an English teacher friend, for her proofreading of this very humble attempt at writing and for her gentle coaching on how to say it more correctly.

Much appreciation is also due Jane Haefner, whose attention to detail and computer expertise produced the final manuscript so efficiently.

Finally, I am forever and lovingly grateful to Frances and to our two sons, Lee and Scott, for allowing me the time, here and there, to put together this book about my Vietnam experiences.

# INTRODUCTION

In the spring of 1966, less than a year after my college graduation, my commissioning as a United States Army second lieutenant, and my marriage, I received orders for Vietnam. Going to war had been a boyhood dream, but the reality was another matter altogether. I suddenly discovered that the prospect of leaving Frances, my wife of only eight months, and perhaps being killed at age 23 or 24 was anything but exciting. Instead, a fear grew within me the likes of which I'd never felt before.

Two months later, on board a troopship and just days before landing on the shore of Vietnam, I wrote to Frances, "Save every one of these letters so that I'll always have a record of what happened." And a day later I also wrote to my folks, "Be sure and save all my letters. When I get home I want to consolidate all my letters to you and Frances into a memoir." What possessed me to contrive such an idea completely escapes me now. Perhaps I feared that my sacrifice, whatever it might be, would be forgotten. Seven months later, in a letter to Frances, I brought up the idea again, this time expanding on it, and apparently never doubting for a moment that I'd make it home to work on the project: "What a job it's going to be someday trying to sort out all my letters, to put everything down into one large diary and at the same time add to [it]. This is something I definitely want to do. Get it all arranged, perfected, and then typed and put in book form, for private use only. If I ever could accomplish this, I might even like to make a couple copies and maybe give one to the folks and your folks. It would give them an idea what a year is like over here, or at least what it was like for me. A pretty good description of my year, I think, is contained in my letters and should be a good basis for a year's running description of events." Ten years afterward—much later than I ever intended—I finally completed the project for my family. And now, later still, those letters and memories have taken new form for an audience I never imagined back in 1966–67.

This book covers April 1966 to May 1967, encompassing most of my experiences from the time I was notified of my impending Vietnam duty until I returned from the war. It contains most of the letters I wrote home to Frances and my folks, plus additional memoirs. The memoirs fill in time gaps between letters, expand on some of the letters themselves, and detail events and experiences I didn't write home about. What I have tried to do throughout is fit letters and memoirs together in an understandable sequence that tells the entire story of my Vietnam experience as I perceived it then and as I recall it now.

The story told is that of an inexperienced field artillery second lieutenant from Nebraska who went to war not because he wanted to but because he was ordered to. It is not an account immersed in anger or dismay about the war; indeed, I accepted service in Vietnam as a patriotic duty and believed the war was necessary while I was there. Unlike many other books on war, mine is not about big battles, heroism, the rightness or wrongness of the war, or horrific combat. It is not written by an accomplished author, West Point graduate, or national hero. Instead, it is the story of a man with no particular claim to fame, an average reserve commissioned officer (like most officers), and of combat from the artilleryman's point of view. In short, it is the story of boredom, discomfort, homesickness, death, rumor, feelings, fear, and many other things encompassing an encounter with war.

Although I consider my war experiences mild compared with those of many who served in Vietnam, at the same time my duty was not without hazard or uniqueness. During my approximately 11 months "in country," I served as an artillery aerial observer, an artillery forward observer (FO), and an artillery battery fire direction officer (FDO). What made these duties unusual was that most of the time my battery supported our Australian and New Zealand allies in Vietnam. I flew with an Australian army aviation outfit and did my forward observing for the New Zealand artillery as well as our own, in support of the Australian infantry and armored cavalry. During these duties, I learned what it is to be shot at, mortared, and mined. And I learned about suffering and death on a small scale, except for one incident that unlike all my experiences before or after, gave me a look at death on a large scale.

Since my experiences were those of an artilleryman, they are for the most part not the high-drama adventures some others may have had. Of course in Vietnam, regardless of service, branch, or job, exposure to combat depended primarily on the enemy's actions in relation to one's own whereabouts. Concerning artillerymen in general, however, apart from the occasional incidents of massive enemy ground attack against artillery units, it has been written that cannoneers led lives that were monotonous and lacking in comfort or diversity. Except for the "comfort" part, this certainly applied to my own artillery battery.

Fortunately or not, depending on how you view it, my role as an artilleryman was more exciting for a time than life was for the cannoneers. As an FO, I was the eyes for the guns and spent five months of my tour flying (spotting), living, and working with the infantry and armored cavalry. My job was to see the target or, more likely, guess where it was, radio its location back to the artillery, and then adjust the fire onto the target. After this duty, however, it was back to my battery as FDO and back to the monotony and sameness of the cannoneers.

In putting this book together, I have omitted a few letters and deleted parts of others that contained information inconsequential to my Vietnam experience. I cut letters and letter segments in which I spoke of personal finances, family activities, the family farm, crops, the weather at home, and so on. I also deleted intimate expressions of love to Frances and my ramblings about the future: career plans, family hopes, and the like. For the most part I cut out duplication between letters to Frances and to my folks, salutations except those necessary for clarity, and all but two closings. A few explanations have been added in brackets. On the whole, however, the letters included have been reproduced as I wrote them, edited only to spare readers or to ensure readability.

There are a few cases in the letters where I have edited out the names of individuals, to avoid hurting feelings or causing embarrassment. Readers will also find that in the memoirs some names are avoided and some first names are absent when they could just as well have been used. The only reason is that I cannot remember them. All in all, missing names and deleted personal communications to family in no way alter or affect the overall tone or meaning of any of my letters or the book in general. All photographs are from my own collection unless otherwise noted.

One final word of explanation. There are portions of a few letters that were based on rumor, exaggeration, or plain misinformation. Where I have been able to recognize such inaccuracies, I have qualified and clarified them in brackets. However, readers should realize that this entire collection of letters and memories represents my perception of what was happening then and what I now recall as having happened. If I have not been entirely successful in my attempt to be clear and objective, it is due only to my own ignorance and inability to see the truth.

# **A**BBREVIATIONS

1ATF = 1st Australian Task Force
1/lt = first lieutenant
2IC = second-in-command
2/lt = second lieutenant
2/35 Arty = 2d Battalion, 35th Artillery
5RAR = 5th Battalion, Royal Australian Regiment
6RAR = 6th Battalion, Royal Australian Regiment
11th ACR = 11th Armored Cavalry Regiment
161 Recce = 161 Reconnaissance Flight
ammo = ammunition
APC = armored personnel carrier
arty = artillery
ARVN = Army of the Republic of Vietnam (South Vietnam)
asst adj. = assistant adjutant
AWOL = absent without leave
BC = battery commander
bn = battalion
BOQ = bachelor officer quarters
btry = battery
cal. = caliber
capt. = captain
Chicom = Chinese Communist
cmdr = commander
CO = commanding officer
col. = colonel
COSVN = Central Office of South Vietnam
Cs = c rations
CSM = company sergeant major
div. = division
EM = enlisted man
FAC = forward air controller (U.S. Air Force)

FDC = Fire Direction Center
FDO = fire direction officer
FO = artillery forward observer
H&I = harassment and interdiction fires
how. = howitzer
HQ = headquarters
inf. = infantry
KIA = killed in action
ldr = leader
lt = lieutenant
LTC = lieutenant colonel
LZ = landing zone
medevac = medical evacuation by helicopter, referred to as "dust off"
mm = millimeter
NATO = North Atlantic Treaty Organization
NCO = noncommissioned officer
NVA = North Vietnamese army
OP = observation post
PFC = private first class
plt. = platoon
PSP = perforated steel plank
pvt. = private
PX = post exchange
R&C = rest and convalescence
R&R = rest and recuperation
recon. = reconnaissance
RNZA = Royal New Zealand Artillery
RPG = rocket-propelled grenade
RSM = regimental sergeant major
RTO = radio telephone operator
SAS = Special Air Service
sgt = sergeant
tgt = target
TOC = Tactical Operations Center
USO = United Service Organizations
VC = Viet Cong
VD = venereal disease
XO = executive officer

# ALLIES AND MATES

# 1. **P**RELUDE

Dearest Frances,                    29 September 66

We just got in from the operation [Operation Vaucluse]. There were times when we were so darn cold and wet and dirty that we all couldn't have cared less if Charlie [short for Victor Charlie, the military communications code words for *V* and *C*, hence Viet Cong] had hit us, and hit us he did. Our third day out Charlie hit us five times. The first time we were just walking along and all of a sudden four vc hit our forward platoon. Then we moved on top of a small ridge and set up camp. About then four more vc walked up to a machine gunner about 30 yds away from us, and all hell broke loose again. After things were calm, we were joking about how we thought there were no vc around. As we shot the bull, Charlie hit us, this time pretty hard. Boy, did I do the fast 40-yard crawl back to my radio and weapon. I've never tried to get so low to the ground in all my life, because the old bullets were really whipping over-head. It's funny, all those times we were hit, not once did I actually see Charlie. All you see is movement in the bushes or something like that. The heck of it is they're shooting at you from about 20 yds. away.

27 December 66

The night before Xmas Eve I volunteered myself and my [fo] section to go out with the infantry on an all-night ambush. Well, about 2 AM five vc walked right in among us. They came up from behind us; we were looking down the trail the opposite direction. We opened up on them from a range of about five feet—you can imagine the panic. You know, it's funny, when you kill a vc it's just like getting your hunting limit of ducks or pheasants. Most of us don't think of vc as humans.

All my love, Gordon

Incidents like these and others, some that I wrote home about and others that I didn't, remain etched in my mind as if they happened yesterday. Through my letters and memories, the war in Vietnam seems almost as real to me today as it was in 1966–67. It's hard to imagine now that the events that took me half a world away began so long ago.

April 1966 was a busy month for me at Fort Carson, Colorado. My battery commander had gone on leave for a couple of weeks, leaving me to prepare the unit loading plans. In addition, our battery was in the middle of training troops, and I had the responsibility of running a .50-caliber machine-gun range. On top of this, battalion headquarters had selected me to act as defense counsel for a soldier who had gone AWOL.

The young private and I worked hard preparing his testimony for the court-martial hearing. On the day of the hearing I spent all morning with him going over how he was to respond to my questions. As we rehearsed his testimony for the final time, a messenger from battalion headquarters arrived and informed me that I was to report to the battalion commander immediately. We finished our hearing preparations rather abruptly, and I hurried over to headquarters.

I entered the battalion CO's office and reported. It seemed he was being unusually nice as he inquired if I had heard that our barracks neighbors to the west, the 2d Battalion 35th Artillery (2/35th), had received orders for movement to Vietnam. Of course I'd heard—everyone on post had! We'd watched them train during the past couple of months, and in recent weeks three of our own battalion officers had been transferred to the 2/35th. As all sorts of thoughts raced through my mind, he told me that the Department of the Army had authorized a special augmentation of six forward observers (FOs) to the 2/35th and that I was to be one of them. He went on to say that immediately after the court-martial hearing I was to report there for assignment and instructions so that I could put my personal affairs in order before departing for Vietnam during the last part of May. Later in the day I learned I would be assigned specifically to A Battery as one of two new battery FOs.

On receiving the news I was speechless, terror-stricken, and dumbfounded. It seemed as if my life had been ruined, all future plans thrown out the window, and whatever I had on my mind wiped out forever. I recovered enough to say "Yes, sir," salute, and stumble out of his office. The news hit me so hard that I left headquarters in a daze. Though my life seemed ended, there still remained a task to accomplish that day—the defense of the young soldier. Somehow I pulled myself together, had lunch, and went through the hearing as planned. We did quite well: the court-martial board gave him a light sentence. The day at least had one bright spot.

The hearing lasted until about 3:00, so I still had two duty hours before going home. Unlike my normal working habits, I said to hell with it all and went home early. Frances was at work and wouldn't be home until after 5, so I spent the rest of the afternoon alone, lying on the bed in our Colorado Springs apartment and thinking about anything and everything relating to the news. Assignment as a forward observer! I had heard stories about FOs and how their life expectancy in combat was about 60 seconds. Actually, I should have known better than to believe such tales. I should have realized that the 60-second story probably originated during World War I, when FOs often observed from balloons above the trench lines, and that during World War II and in Korea observers fared better. Besides, in Vietnam the FO did not go forward; he simply accompanied the infantry. Accompany the infantry! The thought brought wild visions of horror. All I could think of was the big Vietnam battle of November 1965 in which the 1st Cavalry Division (Airmobile) had run into a large force in the Ia Drang Valley and lost close to 300 men while killing nearly 2,000 of the enemy. This battle had received tremendous coverage in the newspapers, especially in cities near army posts. I guess it seemed exceptionally significant at the time because it was the first really large-scale battle U.S. forces had been involved in since American combat units were first committed in March 1965.

I lay there wondering if I would survive or whether Frances would end up a widow at 23 or 24. I prayed, remembered the stories Dad had told about World War II on Saipan and Iwo Jima, wondered how I would react under fire, and thought of those days 10 years earlier when my fondest boyhood dream was to be a soldier. I thought of all the previous "crises" I had endured—the biggest high-school football and basketball games of the year, whether I could get a date for the fraternity's spring formal, and

3

how I had worried about college hour exams and finals. They all seemed foolish compared with what I faced now.

It was probably a good thing I had a little time by myself to think things over. In the two hours before Frances came home I managed to come to terms with the situation and resolved to make the best of it. After all, millions before me had faced the same possibilities but had accepted them and served. It would be no different with me. If I had to die at this age, then so be it. At least, I reasoned, it would be a more honorable death than being killed in an auto accident. Besides, hadn't President Kennedy said some years ago that we would "pay any price . . . oppose any foe"? I believed in that. By the time Frances got home I had accepted my plight, convincing myself that my destiny very simply lay in the hands of God.

When Frances arrived I told her the news. It was an emotional moment, but soon we began to plan for the coming year. It was quickly settled that she would return with me to Colorado Springs after my leave at home and see me off on the last day. We also decided that during the year she would live with her folks back home in Nebraska and try to get a teaching job. Then, too, there was the task of telling our parents. I wrote to mine the next day.

> Dear Folks,                                    21 April 66
> I'm afraid this will be a rather unpleasant letter. I got the bad word yesterday that I'm going to Vietnam. The worst part of it is the short notice. We (our bn) leave from here (Fort Carson) about May 24th for San Francisco and from there by ship across the ocean. We'll probably arrive in Vietnam about the middle or end of June.
> I suppose this is pretty much of a shock to you. I knew it was just a matter of time until I had to go, but I sure didn't think it would be this soon. Needless to say I don't want to go, but guess I've got my duty, and so I'll do it the best I can. There's only one way to look at it now; apparently the good Lord wants me there for some reason, and you just don't dispute that.

This very memorable letter written, we set about doing what had to be done. During the next few days I had my will prepared, signed a power of attorney, wrapped up my affairs at my old unit of two months, and reported in to my new unit, A Battery, 2d Battalion, 35th Artillery, a 155-mm self-propelled (M109) howitzer outfit.

4

I reported in to A Battery and there met one of the most interesting characters I've ever run across, my new battery commander, Captain Glenn Eure. Captain Eure was short and muscular, carried either a smile or a scowl, and wore more badges and
tabs on his fatigues than I'd ever seen before. He was a Korean
War veteran and veteran of one tour of duty in Vietnam as a Military Assistance Command Vietnam adviser. He was likable, funny,
overbearing, and authoritative, all rolled into one short stack of
pure military. All in all, Eure was the kind of commander a green-
horn like me needed at this stage. Though less than a month
remained before deployment, he had everyone believing that the
whole affair would come out all right for us: all we had to do was
stick with him.

One thing for sure, we were determined to take every possible
convenience with us. We loaded refrigerators and a TV set on one
of the trucks that was to be tarped, banded, and sealed before
shipment. We loaded toilet seats, plumbing parts, and all sorts of
items into vehicles and conex containers. All the while we toiled
getting ready for the move, Eure favored whomever he chose at
the moment with pearls of country wisdom: "May the bird of
paradise fly up your nose," or "Buy you books and buy you books,
and what do you do? Eat them!" or "Son, you look happier than a
pig wallowing in shit!" That was Captain Eure, always encourag-
ing, being funny, or just purely raising hell.

Eure also had another side. He could sit for hours strumming
his guitar, reciting old military poems, and singing barracks bal-
lads. Within the battery itself and among the men, he was a wonder. He knew everyone by name, though most were new and had
come to the battalion only weeks before, fresh from training. He
was tuned in to the heartbeat of the unit and had succeeded in
convincing everyone, me included, that we would do a great job
in Vietnam. In the few days I spent with the battery before going
home on leave, he quieted many of my fears about the year to
come simply by being the dynamic and confident officer he was.
If he feared Vietnam at all, it wasn't noticeable. He gave the im-
pression that we were about to embark on a great crusade, one he
looked forward to with pleasure.

I found the other officers of the battery to be as likable as Captain Eure. The battery executive officer First Lieutenant Harold

Grace, a Kansas native, was quiet, unassuming, and easygoing but got his job done. His situation was rather unfortunate. He had less than six months left to serve in the army, and his wife was expecting their first child about the end of May, just when we were to depart for Vietnam. But 1966 was the year of the big buildup, and so officers like Harold Grace went too for the few months they had left in the army.

Our battery fire direction officer was Second Lieutenant Chuck Heindrichs, a West Point graduate. Where Harold was quiet, Chuck was loud, obnoxious, and at times overbearing. Though he had no formal artillery gunnery schooling, Chuck taught himself, and with the help of the FDC section chief, Sergeant First Class Hicks, he molded the Fire Direction Center into a capable organization. At handling troops, Chuck was a wizard. He could be loud and harsh one moment and the next minute put his arm around a soldier and say, "OK, now let's sort this problem out." Like Eure, Chuck had a gift for keeping morale high. Also like Captain Eure, Chuck played the guitar, a talent all of us were to appreciate in the coming months.

The other battery FO besides me was Second Lieutenant Roy Minick from Vermont. Roy was the absolute stereotype of the Vermonter. His humor was dry, and he spoke crisply and little. He had graduated from Dartmouth with a major in English and earned his commission through officer candidate school at Fort Sill, Oklahoma. Three of us were married, and Chuck and Roy were single.

Of the 30 or so officers in the 2/35th, I was the most junior. As the newest and perhaps greenest of all, I could expect to draw the dirtiest assignments. I once spoke to the battalion S3 (operations officer) about this and mentioned that I was the only married officer among the FOs in the battalion. I was trying to suggest that perhaps an unmarried second lieutenant might be better suited for the dangerous job of FO. The S3 ignored my hint and told me in no uncertain terms that since I was the junior officer in the battalion, not much could be done until a more junior officer was assigned. One never was, so I spent my entire year in Vietnam as the junior officer, first as a second lieutenant and later, when promotions came, as junior first lieutenant. One might think that with casualties and sickness this would have changed, but every replacement officer the battalion took in during the year was my senior. Not until the last days before my return home, when my own replacement arrived, was there any officer in the battalion junior to me.

Before Frances and I left Fort Carson to go home on leave, Captain Eure and his wife graciously invited the A Battery officers and their ladies to his home for a farewell dinner. It was a bittersweet affair in that for Roy, Frances, and me it was the first and last social gathering of this kind. After dinner we sang songs while Chuck and Eure played their guitars. We closed the evening by looking at photographs Eure had taken during his first tour of duty in Vietnam. I had the distinct feeling that few enjoyed this part of the evening.

The final planned activity before all of us in the battalion left Fort Carson to go on leave was a formal parade and inspection by the post commander and commander of the 5th Infantry Division (Mechanized). The general "trooped the line" and then got down from his review jeep and walked through the ranks, talking to a few of the men. He stopped within our battery and talked to a young Mexican American. This particular man was serving in the army to speed up receiving his citizenship. The general asked him, "Why are you going to Vietnam, son?" To everyone's amazement he replied, "To kill vc, sir!"

With equipment packed, training done, and final parade and review completed, all of us were given our last instructions—take leave and return to Fort Carson for final assembly and briefing before departing for Vietnam (somewhere in Southeast Asia, they said then) on 27 May. I was happy to go on leave but regretted that I had not had the opportunity to train with the battalion. Worse, I dreaded saying good-bye to everyone back home at the end of my short leave—17 days that I knew would go all too fast.

During the days I spent back home in Nebraska, family gatherings were arranged, though my choice would have been none at all. Frances's family assembled to say their good-byes at her parents' farm home. Her folks, like mine, were typical eastern Nebraska farmers with a small herd of dairy cows, a few feeder cattle, hogs, and of course a flock of chickens. Wheat, corn, milo, and alfalfa were their main crops, and like my parents, just 40 miles to the west, they were devout, churchgoing Lutherans. Despite these comfortable and familiar surroundings, the whole affair seemed awkward. Everyone avoided the subject of Vietnam until the final farewell as, family by family, they took their leave of us. Generally everyone was at a loss for words. What could they say? "Be careful!" "Don't take any chances!" "Don't volunteer for anything!" I guess most of them simply said "Good luck!"

My own aunts, uncles, and cousins gathered at Grandma Endorf's home. Once again the subject of Vietnam was generally ignored except that, ironically, someone had turned on the TV and on that afternoon one of the networks was running a special on an infantry company of the 1st Cavalry Division (Airmobile) and what it was like for them in Vietnam. As we visited that day one of my aunts, in her typically straightforward fashion, asked me, "Well, what good do you think you'll do over there?"

Apart from family gatherings, the days of leave were pleasant enough. Having time to putter around the Steinbrook family farm and be with Mom, Dad, and my sister, Mary Jean, was probably good therapy. It also allowed me time to just drive around and look at the farms and fields south of Tobias, Nebraska, that had been home to me all my life except for my years at the university in Lincoln. I wondered if it would be my last look. I'm not sure I had ever realized until then how much I loved my little community, started by half a dozen German Lutheran families in the 1870s, with a sprinkling of other nationalities and religions all around and a sizable Czech population nearby. The big white Missouri Synod Lutheran church at the center, surrounded by fields of wheat, corn, and milo, and the nearby parochial schoolhouse were the focal points. I'd attended that little two-room country school for eight years before entering public high school and had probably missed church only once in my life. It was a very tightly knit religious community that I'd been eager to leave after high school, but now I would have given anything to stay.

At last we came to the end of my leave and the time I dreaded most—saying good-bye to my folks. We were packed, had the car loaded, and stood on the south farmhouse sidewalk near the yard gate, ready to say our final farewells. I kissed and hugged Mom and Mary Jean and shook hands with Dad. At the last moment Dad grabbed and hugged me; he was all choked up and maybe even crying. In that instant I realized that of all the family members only he, a veteran of World War II, knew what I might face during the next year. For me as I hugged Dad, all the strain and emotion finally came to a head. Tears welled up so I could barely find my way to the car. As I drove down the farmstead lane, tears continued to flow. Turning onto the country road, I drove many miles in a tearful fog. Without question that final farewell ranks as one of the most difficult, emotional, and memorable events of my life.

Leave, though welcome, had been hard for me. The only bright spot was that Frances got a teaching job for the coming year. A graduate of Peru State Teachers College in Nebraska, she already had two years' teaching experience. She would be busy with her third- and fourth-grade class at Pickrell, a little town a few miles from Beatrice and from her parents' farm, where she'd be living for the next twelve months. And other things would keep her occupied. She planned to teach Sunday school, sing in the church choir, and take some college classes. There would also be family activities with her parents, brother, sister and brother-in-law, three nieces, and all her aunts, uncles, and cousins, not to mention my family nearby. She'd be all right, and the year would go fast for her, I prayed. I only hoped it would pass quickly for me as well.

Having made the one-day drive back to Colorado Springs, we spent those last days mostly doing nothing. I checked in with A Battery occasionally for any final instructions, but for the most part I concentrated on packing and just being with Frances. The afternoon and evening of the last day, however, I will never forget. Since Frances and I had not been able to take communion at home before we left, we called our local minister and asked if he would come to our apartment so we could receive it there. He agreed and came over. For me it was a tremendous comfort and spiritual lift to take communion on that very last day.

That night Frances and I went to a drive-in movie and saw *The Pink Panther,* for probably the fourth time. It wasn't that we really wanted to see that movie—or any movie—it simply filled the time before I had to go.

Our battalion was to leave Colorado Springs about 7:00 A.M. from the city airport. From there we would fly to Oakland, California, and board the troopship. Our orders were to be in the battery area that morning by 4:30. Frances and I slept little if at all that night. I had arranged for a taxi to pick me up at 4:00 and take me to Fort Carson, to spare Frances the ordeal of having to drive back home after seeing me off. As the time approached and we sat there waiting to say a final good-bye for a whole year, emotions again began to well up, as they had when I left my parents. We began to cry and embrace, knowing this was it. It all seemed so tragic—we had been married for only eight months.

The taxi arrived, and the driver honked. A final good-bye kiss and embrace, some fumbling with my baggage, and out into the dark, crisp mountain air I went, crying as I hadn't cried since age 12 when my Grandma Steinbrook died. Down the stairs from our balcony I went, struggling with the bags. The driver helped me load them and, still crying, I climbed into the backseat. One final wave to Frances standing at the window and we were gone.

The ride to Fort Carson gave me time to pull myself together and brace myself for the officer role I would have to play from there on out. As we got to the battery area I could see others arriving in the dim light, many with entire families and pets tagging along for the final farewell. I unloaded my bags, paid the cabbie, and went to the orderly room. Good mornings were said as though it were just another workday—"Good morning, sir!" "Good morning, First Sergeant!" The coffee was on, and for the first of many times during the next year out came the canteen cup, in went a spoonful of sugar and a heavy dose of Pet evaporated milk, and finally that hot and unique army coffee.

We sat around for what seemed hours waiting for the troops to gather. When they had all arrived, we drew our weapons from the arms room and assembled in formation out on the street. As we waited for the buses that would take us to the airport, the Fort Carson post band pulled up in its bus and parked across the street. They drew up in the parking area, and as we waited they played military music. Our buses arrived and we boarded, then as we pulled away toward the airport, the band played "Auld Lang Syne." I could hear several men in the bus stifle sobs. As for me, the officer image almost gave way to what everyone on that bus really wanted to do.

In less than 30 minutes our buses pulled into the airport. We off-loaded, milled around a bit, collected our baggage, and then walked toward the runway to board the waiting aircraft. I was surprised to see that we would travel by chartered civilian jet-liners, instead of military planes. To the civilian onlookers we must have been quite a sight: over 500 men all clad in fatigues and helmets and carrying our weapons as we boarded those airliners and were welcomed by flight attendants. I remember feeling silly sitting in my seat holding my rifle while a good-looking little stewardess asked if there was anything she could do for me. I also remember thinking that from now on my only contact with home would be by letters, first from on board ship and, for the rest of the year, I hoped, from Vietnam.

Dear Folks,                                    27 May 66

I left Colo. Springs this morning by plane at 7:00. By 11:00 we were all aboard ship.

We're on a U.S. Navy troop transport. It's fairly new; however, it's also fairly small. About the most people it will hold is 3,000, and of course we're loaded to the gills. The troops are on about the third or fourth deck below the top deck. They're crammed in there like sardines with bunks stacked up to the ceilings. I bet the top bunk must be nine or 10 feet off the floor. I'm in a very small room with three other lts., but in not too long there will probably be 12 of us in here.

Dearest Frances,                              27 May 66

Our ship leaves tomorrow afternoon at 2:00 for Seattle. The word is we might be on ship for almost a month.

Our quarters are a little tight. We're as bad off as the rest of the troops, practically. At least we have a porthole in our room. That's more than most of the other officers have. Without that porthole their rooms are really hot.

The food in the navy officers' mess is tremendous. The navy sure does eat good. It's like eating in a restaurant with waiters, etc. Guess I should have been a naval officer.

Our ship pulled out the next day, 28 May, as a navy band stood in formation on the dock playing "I Left My Heart in San Francisco." I'm not sure what those bands were trying to do to us. First "Auld Lang Syne" at Fort Carson, and now this. The ship moved fairly fast for its size, I thought, and in no time we were out in the middle of the harbor passing old Alcatraz prison and finally going under the fog-covered Golden Gate Bridge. Steaming under the bridge brought visions of World War II. I think every war movie I'd ever seen set in the Pacific Theater had a scene of the troops passing beneath that bridge.

Dearest Frances,                                              30 May 66
    In a couple of more hours we'll be pulling into Tacoma, Washington. The trip from San Francisco to here has been a real bitch. We had heavy seas all the way. Our ship has been jumping like a teeter-totter, up and down, up and down. Then last night we started rolling sideways. I tell you, I'll never travel by ship again. Most everyone is somewhat sick. I think all of us spend about 90% of the time in bed. The boredom here is terrible. There's absolutely nothing to do, and as far as that goes no one's well enough to do anything. Well one good thing, the sea is getting smoother now that we're pulling into port. You know, the worst thing about the rough water was that a person could hardly stand up, let alone walk. I sure didn't think the ocean would whip a big ship around as easily as it did. Well, only 15–20 more days of this. I'll be glad when we get to Vietnam just to get off this tub.
    You know, I still can't believe this whole situation. It's still like a big dream. I don't really think I'll wake up until one year from now, and then I'll still never believe it happened.
                                                             1 June 66
    This morning we left [Tacoma] almost on schedule, headed north up out of the Puget Sound and back south once more into open sea. We really don't have any idea of our route, but since we're going almost straight south now I'd say we're heading straight for Vietnam. If that's the case and we don't stop anywhere, I imagine we'll be there by the middle of June.
    Once we got back out into open sea this old ship started rocking again, but not like before. Unless we hit heavy water I don't think it will trouble me anymore. One thing you just can't imagine, the sun doesn't set until about 9:30 P.M. It's really kind of weird but awfully beautiful. Here it's time to go to bed and the sun has just gone down. The ocean kind of fascinates me. It's so big and terrible looking, but I kind of like it.
                                                             5 June 66
    Our battalion will be the last to get off the ship. We make three stops once we get there, and we get off on the third stop. So for three days plus or minus we'll cruise along offshore. I guess there will be some element of danger in doing this. They told us to

keep our portholes shut so the VC can't toss hand grenades in. Once we get on shore we have to go by convoy to our area, wherever that is. This also could be a little hairy.

I know our route for sure now. If you look at a world map, it's just a straight line between Tacoma and Vietnam. We pass north of the Hawaiian Is., south of Formosa, and north of the Philippines. We come within just a few miles of the island of Iwo Jima, one of the islands Dad was on.

12 June 66

It's been awhile since I've last written. We have been training, and really that's all that's been happening. I just don't know what to write, so I just put off writing altogether. Maybe I almost hate to write because then I think of you and I get so lonely.

Every day now gets hotter. Really the heat isn't bad so far, only about 80 to 85°, but the humidity must be in the 90s. In a day or so we'll be going past Formosa, Bataan, the Philippines, and into the South China Sea. That's when the heat and humidity will really start to pick up.

I guess we're scheduled to arrive in Vietnam Thurs. morning for our first stop. We probably won't get off until about Sat. or Sun. According to what we've been told as of today, we'll load on flatboats from the ship, from there onto amphibious landing craft, and then hit the beach. From there we go by helicopter to our equipment and into our position. I guess quite a number of our people will be transferred to other units when we get there, so that one year from now not everyone will leave at once. Some from our unit will be traded for people that have already been there awhile.

Tomorrow we start taking malaria pills. Big news, huh? Well such is a big event with us. We had a real nice church service on ship this morning. You'd be surprised how many people go to services. I got a haircut yesterday. Almost everyone is growing a mustache except me. Right now I just can't see it. Maybe later on I'll grow one.

It's hard to believe that when we get there we will have been on this ship for three weeks. Exactly one year ago today I graduated [from the university] and got my commission.

15 June 66

We should arrive tomorrow morning at our first stop. I can't really say if I'm excited, scared, or what. I really don't think I'm either. I'm kind of indifferent with one or two things in mind, to keep myself and my FO party healthy and do a good job. What I find hard to believe is that if I just do an acceptable job and not a good job I'm still responsible for killing hundreds of people during the next year. Can you imagine me a killer? Well really, I guess I'm a paid killer. I get $400 clear every month just for that. Really, I don't think of myself like I just said. On the other hand, I tend to think of myself as a patriot in defense of freedom like thousands before me. Just think how many men in the world have gone to war since the beginning of time.

16 June 66, 11:15 P.M.

At 2 P.M. today we arrived at our first stop. We stopped at a place that was unscheduled, so now we've still got three more to make before we get off. We're at a place called Qui Nhon, supposedly a very secure port. Well tonight we know what a secure port is like. We can hear artillery fire in the distance rumble like thunder and see the flashes against the sky. Our ship guards are walking around with live ammo in their rifles, and we've got spotlights burning on the ship all around us so that no boat can approach without being seen. Some of the units get off here, so they have sent guards to shore to secure an area. I imagine those particular people are shook up tonight out in the dark.

The sight of the country here is unbelievable. There's a high mountain range all along the coast, covered with heavy jungle. I know it's heavy because I've been studying it with my binos [binoculars] all day. It's hard to imagine we're here, but that jungle looks pretty convincing.

As we were coming in, little fishing boats were thick all around us. Those boats have sails and a crew of four or five people. They are either junks or sampans. The first one we passed really made me realize where we are. There were four Vietnamese in it dressed in black pajamas and white coolie hats. Of course this is supposedly the VC dress, however, we have been told all along that the good guys also wear this same outfit. So as you can see, the problem is to tell who is who. One of our sgts. who had already been here once said that the only way you can tell is when they shoot at you. Nice way of identification, huh?

I think the reality of this thing is finally beginning to get to everyone. Everyone is beginning to worry a little, me included. That dark jungle looks pretty horrible from a distance. Think how

14

bad it must be from within. Actually, this whole thing is like a war movie. We've even got the typical war movie characters! Among the officers we have two farmers (counting myself), a couple from good New England families, one from Brooklyn, one from the Bronx, and a couple from the windy city of Chicago. The one from Brooklyn is even Italian, to top everything off. Quite a crew of officers—actually a group of kids. This is where we differ from the movies. In the movies the officers are always experienced older soldiers. In our cast it's just the opposite, but probably more realistic.

Tonight our movie was *To Kill a Man*, a Vietnam war movie. What an ungodly movie to have at this point in the game. Well I guess we all enjoyed it though, regardless. You'd be surprised at our sense of humor on this whole matter of Vietnam. To us I guess it's a way of hiding or maybe bringing out our feelings. To anyone else than us it probably wouldn't be humorous at all.

I've succeeded in training my FO section pretty well. I've even struck up a pretty good friendship with Pvt. [Jim] Gleason, my RTO. In fact we're probably better friends than I am with any of the officers, although they are pretty great guys. Of course since I'll be working with Pvt. Gleason night and day we might as well be the best of friends. Actually, he seems to have the same background as myself: born on a small farm in Wash., likes hunting, is married (wife expecting, four months along), hometown of about 800, graduated from high school in 1960, and so on. I guess the thing I like best about him is that he's so darn honest and sincere about everything. One other thing I like about Gleason is that he and I have the same blood type. This could prove advantageous to one or another at some time.

20 June 66

We're still sitting here on ship in the harbor at Qui Nhon. We were supposed to leave for our second port last Fri., but it didn't come off. As it stands now we leave tomorrow morning. Of course we don't know for sure. Last Fri. one artillery unit did get off and went to Nha Trang. This was supposed to be our next stop, but I guess as soon as they got there (Nha Trang) (within 24 hours) they were under fire already. They don't even have their equipment with them. They just have rifles. So as a result of this it's too hot for us to dock there, so we'll move on to a different harbor.

The last couple of mornings have been somewhat exciting. A couple of boatloads of women (Vietnamese types) tried to board us. The first groups were held off by our water hoses, but the second group was shot at by us. Needless to say, they left. Then last night there were some more rifles firing around us, but we don't know what it was for.

Monday evening

We moved out tonight heading south. We think we're going to Cam Ranh Bay. After being out about an hour, and still at the present, the artillery on the coast started putting on a real show. They're shooting illumination rounds that light up the whole coastline and then follow that with high explosive shells (HE). It's just like the Fourth of July.

22 June 66

Today we got the scoop on what we'll be doing. As it stands now I will certainly be an FO and probably observe about 90% from a spotter plane and the other 10% from the ground being attached to the infantry. As soon as we land, probably tomorrow or the next day, we'll all move to a staging area north of Saigon and there get our equipment in shape for travel. Then the battalion will split up, each btry going its separate way. All of the btrys except for us are supporting a Vietnamese division. We'll be southeast of Saigon with an Australian infantry regiment [the 1st Australian Task Force actually]. So none of us will be working with American infantry units like we all figured. Right now the only other arty units in our area are one unit of Australian arty and one unit of New Zealand arty. I guess later on a couple more American arty units will join us. Until the other American units join us we'll have the heaviest cal. arty in the area.

All of us are real happy about joining the Australians rather than the Vietnamese div. At least we'll know who our friends are. Not only that, but the Australians are an elite group especially trained and sent to Vietnam for this type of war. Rumor has it that they are tremendous fighters and actually better soldiers man for man than the American soldier in Vietnam. I just can't say how pleased I am to be going to such an elite group of men. Of course this will be quite an experience for us. We'll have to get used to their rough and tough methods of doing things. From what I understand, they are truly professional hard-core type people, and because of this we'll have to work our butts off to keep up with them.

By the way, save every one of these letters so that I'll always have a record of what happened. When I get home I intend to combine all this into a memoir.

Dearest Frances,                                    23 June 66, 10:30 P.M.

Tomorrow morning we get off the ship, and then the fun begins. We'll unload at the port [Vung Tau] and then fly to Bien Hoa, our staging area, where we'll collect our equipment and train before we move out to our designated areas of responsibility. We'll probably be there for at least a week, maybe more. Not too long after we get there we expect to be hit. This is the common thing for the VC to do. They like to feel a new unit out as soon as they arrive. They'll run into trouble though if they do hit us. The 173d Airborne will be protecting us in addition to us protecting ourselves. Then from there we have to move all of our equipment by convoy to where we're going. This too will be a critical time. Once we get to our destination we'll be relatively safe as anyone can be over here.

Have I told you that it's possible to take the seven-day rest from combat [R&R] in Hawaii now? Well it is. Who knows, maybe if things worked out right we could meet there during your Christmas vacation. I also get three other choices of areas to spend this time, Bangkok, Hong Kong, and Tokyo. Of course if my seven days doesn't fall during your [school] vacation then I go to one of these places.

I'd best get my rest tonight. I guess it's hard to sleep that first night in Vietnam.

Sleep had come quickly the night before. Knowing that A Battery would be assigned to the 1st Australian Task Force (1ATF) instead of a South Vietnamese infantry division put me at ease. The rest of the battalion was envious of us, and I believe some of the officers would have traded their positions for ours in A Battery just for the chance to work with the Aussies.

The Australians, our staunch allies, had sent advisers to South Vietnam as early as 1962. By 1965 they had committed an infantry battalion and other elements. Also in 1965 New Zealand, another of our allies, had sent an artillery battery of six howitzers to support the Aussie infantry. Together the Aussies and New Zealanders

(Kiwis) worked with the 173d Airborne Brigade out of Bien Hoa on operations in War Zone D, the Iron Triangle. By June 1966, however, the Australians had increased their commitment substantially and were now operating on their own. Their logistical base was at Vung Tau, our port of entry, and the 1st Australian Task Force, consisting of two infantry battalions, Aussie and New Zealand artillery, an armored cavalry squadron, a Special Air Service squadron, and more had established a base camp 40 miles or so southeast of Saigon in Phuoc Tuy Province. From this base camp at a place called Nui Dat, a hill in that vicinity, 1ATF was beginning to conduct operations. It was to Nui Dat and the 1ATF that A Battery and I were to go after staging at Bien Hoa.

With excitement about working with the Aussies on hold, most of us spent hours packing, repacking, and checking our gear again and again that last night on board ship. When I finally did turn in, tired as I was, I couldn't sleep. Whether it was fear, excitement, anticipation, or a combination of all, I lay awake for what seemed hours. At dawn's first light, or perhaps even before, we were all up collecting our bags and donning our personal equipment. Then we waited. We waited to be called up on deck, we waited on deck for our turn to board the barge lying alongside the ship, and then we waited again on the barge for our navy landing craft to arrive.

The landing craft finally pulled alongside and we scrambled aboard, dreading the final leg of our journey yet anxious to reach shore. As our craft churned its way through Vung Tau harbor toward the beaches of Vung Tau itself, my imagination ran wild. Though our landing was supposed to be unopposed and the beach secure, all I could think of was those beach landings of World War II. Since we hadn't been issued ammunition, I prayed that my fears wouldn't materialize.

## 2. STAGING AT BIEN HOA

In view of my fears, our landing was anticlimactic. Charlie wasn't waiting for us on the beach as I had imagined. Instead, trucks and drivers stood ready to take us the short distance to an airfield where air force cargo planes waited to fly our entire battalion to Bien Hoa, site of our staging area. The flight from Vung Tau to Bien Hoa was not anxiety-free; I fully expected our aircraft to be riddled by ground fire either as we took off or as we landed. But nothing happened, and we made the trip without incident. Throughout the year I always seemed to expect the worst, though I never revealed these constant fears in my letters home.

At the staging area our advance party had the tents up and ready for us. The advance party had stayed behind at Fort Carson to finish closing down the battalion area and then had flown to Vietnam ahead of us to prepare our staging area. As we dismounted from the vehicles that had brought us from Bien Hoa Air Force Base to the staging area, we were greeted by Chuck Heindrichs and Harold Grace, A Battery's advance-party officers. Roy Minick and I walked over to the A Battery lieutenants' tent with them as the troops moved to their designated areas. Chuck talked a mile a minute on the way, telling us about the advance party's Vietnam adventures and describing the situation here in the staging area. The situation was excellent if our tent was any indication. Cots were already set up, lawn chairs were sitting here and there, and the focal point, a small ice chest filled with cold beer and soda pop, stood in the center of the tent. Harold and Chuck had, it appeared, stimulated the local economy in getting ready for us. Our temporary home even had a new radio hanging from the center pole blaring the top tunes of the day via Armed Forces Radio.

Dearest Frances,                                    24 June 66

I've spent one day in Vietnam (in country). We hit the shore with landing craft yesterday afternoon at 2:00 P.M. From there we boarded planes and flew to the airport at Bien Hoa [Air Force Base] and from there by truck convoy to our battalion temporary base camp. We arrived here at about 4:30 P.M.

We're located next to the 173d Airborne base camp, which is about a mile from [Bien Hoa] Air Force Base. Four miles north of the edge of our base camp is War Zone D, the Iron Triangle. This is a VC-infested area. In this four-mile zone between us and the Iron Triangle the 173d puts out ambush patrols every night. Last night they got ambushed and had to call in helicopter support. The whole sky to the north of us was ablaze with tracers and flares. You can't imagine how pretty it was.

You'd never believe it, but I'm sitting here drinking an ice-cold beer as I write you. Yes, such is the war here. As long as we're in any kind of a base camp we'll have a few comforts.

Even though most of us feel pretty safe, there's a lot of action going on around us. Just as I'm sitting here I can hear rifle, machine-gun, and artillery [fire], and planes all around me. One of our sgts. got a bullet hole put through his jeep windshield, too, so even though it seems peaceful it's really not.

It's so darn hot, and it will probably rain again soon. It rains about an hour every day. All I can think of is the possibility of us being together at Christmas. Of course that all depends on when I get my R&R. Write, honey; I still haven't gotten any mail from you.

Dear Folks and Mary Jean,        Sun. 26 June 66, 10:00 A.M.

Today is our fourth day in country. As of yet there have been no problems. We're located in a staging area just north of Bien Hoa about a mile, which is about 30 miles north of Saigon. The 173d Airborne base camp is about 100 meters south of us, a Hawk missile site to our west about 100 meters, and open jungle partially bulldozed out to our north front. Like I said, so far no action, except for small arms and arty fire we can hear all around us. So far it just seems like a big outdoor training area in the States.

This morning we had church service with an altar (makeshift) on top of a 50-gallon barrel. The chaplain was a full bird col. that's been in the Pacific during WWII, the Korean War, and two different tours in Vietnam. He's quite a guy, but I can't say too much for his sermon. Of course church doesn't seem like church over here anyway.

My dear sweet wife,                    Sun. 26 June 66, 11:30 A.M.

Have you gotten any of my mail yet? I hope so. I still haven't gotten anything from you or the folks, and I figure it's about a week and three days since I sent my first letter from Vietnam.

Let me tell you what my job is going to be like with the Australians. My FOing will be almost if not entirely from the air, about four hours each day. The rest of the time I'll be doubling as a fire direction officer, security officer, and a number of other things. We're also getting another officer in our battery, which will give us six officers. You see, we have to operate 24 hours a day in shifts, so we need more men.

Yesterday we dug mortar pits so that if we do get hit we'll have some protection.

Tues. 28 June 66, 9:00 A.M.

Yesterday was a happy day for me. I got seven of your letters. They made me feel so good I just couldn't believe it.

The last couple of days have been rather miserable. It's been raining, and it's so darn muddy. The tent leaks, and we can't keep anything dry. Sleeping is a son of a gun, and the mosquitoes are getting worse.

I'm not so sure sometimes that I'll stay in A Btry. One of the senior 2/lts. wants to go with A Btry pretty bad, and since I'm a junior lt. I may just get put out into another battery. If I could trade even with this other guy I'd probably go to headquarters as a full-time air observer, which I wouldn't mind in the least bit. Well, we'll just have to wait and see. Maybe it would be the best after all, because Capt. Eure says that the FOs will probably stay on the ground with the Australians, contrary to what most of us have been told by other people. Frankly, I'm to the point where I couldn't care less. This sitting around is awfully boring. The word is that we'll be here until about the 15th of July. During this time (we've already started) we're trying to beg, borrow, or steal building materials for our base camp [at Nui Dat with the Australians and New Zealanders]. They don't have anything over here. If you want something you've got to know someone or you just don't get it.

Our trucks and other vehicles aren't here yet, so we borrow from other units what we need. When we do go downtown we have to go heavily armed because not everyone's friendly, even the little five- and six-year-old kids can't be trusted.

Speaking of downtown, I haven't been there yet. Those that have say it's really something. The American soldier as always corrupts where he goes. For example, the kids as well as the grownups pick up their knowledge of the English language just from what they hear, consequently kids say, "You number one GI," "you number one zero GI," "you number one f--king GI." Well, you see what I mean.

30 June 66

Today has been a hot, rainless day. We're still in the process of gathering together building materials to take with us. Once we get down there we won't be able to get much of anything. Cement is the hardest thing to come by. When we get to Baria [actually Nui Dat, nine kilometers northeast of Baria (Phuoc Le), the capital of Phuoc Tuy Province], there will be nothing waiting for us except cleared jungle.

Yesterday I went downtown Bien Hoa for the first time. It was a big thrill but also kind of scary. Traffic here is out of this world. People pass you on the left, right, and all which ways all the time you're trying to dodge people and kids on foot, in carts, and on bikes. To give you an idea of how wild driving is here, let me tell you one thing that happened yesterday. We were going down the road about 30 miles an hour through a crowded district when suddenly we realized we were following a car that was going in reverse.

1 July 66

Last night was rather exciting. The 173d that's guarding our north perimeter ran into some VC. They got two out of the six. The two they killed were carrying 105-mm artillery shells probably for use as mines, so today we're being careful about these things. We also thought we might get hit by mortars last night, but we didn't. We were all sleeping in fatigue pants and boots with rifles close at hand, ready to jump at the first thud of a mortar shell. We're all getting a little jumpy, needless to say.

Yesterday at Xuan Loc, the area that HQ, B, and C [batteries] are moving into, the 173d was clearing the area and ran into an ambush. The VC wiped out a 173d platoon of over 40 men. Between Xuan Loc and A's area of Baria there's an estimated 8,000 VC mass-ing. This is one of the reasons why we're going to our particular areas, to try and clear this concentration of vc.

Once we get to Baria we have to send out a night patrol on our perimeter every night of seven men, one NCO and six other EM; however, the first five patrols will be led by an officer in the battery. Capt. Eure is taking the first one out and then the rest of us in order. Looks like we'll get to play infantry too while we're here. I'm not particularly looking forward to this, but then what difference does it really make?

The mosquitoes are getting worse now. Last night most of us got bit up pretty bad. Yesterday I got three more letters from you. They sure do raise my morale.

Dear Folks and Mary Jean,                    2 July 66

I've been in country now for nine days or so, and everything has been peaceful in our staging area here at Bien Hoa. I've been downtown Bien Hoa a few times by now and have had a look at the people and so on. Things are pretty dirty here, with people running all over. The streets are narrow and crowded with traffic jams, etc. A person gets the weirdest feeling driving to town and then around in town. Of course most of the town is off limits because it's unsecure. The mile to town is a dirt road through a kind of swampy area with water standing all over. All along the road are guard posts in bunkers built with sandbags manned by the air force, the 173d Airborne, and Vietnamese soldiers. Many of these guard posts are in old concrete pillboxes dating back to the French occupation, and I would imagine some even date back to the Japanese occupation during WWII. Believe it or not, there are a lot of old Jap minefields still here from WWII, some of them unmarked.

The people here are small, brown, and slant-eyed. They're just a little different than a Chinese or Japanese. I certainly don't trust any of them, though. About 90% of the men wear black pajamas, so the old idea that vc wear black pajamas as a uniform is not true. Of course vc wear them, but so does everyone else, so you can't tell friend from foe until they shoot at you, unless of course you run into some North Vietnamese regulars.

We've received word here that several more units from the States are coming here before the first of next year or shortly after. In a couple of months we'll be joined at the Australians' position by a 175-mm gun battery. Today General Westmoreland said we're winning the war, and a colonel at Xuan Loc said it would be over by March. Now the bombing has begun on Hanoi, so maybe they're right. I sure hope so. I'd love to be a part of the forces that put an end to all this. Last night we heard on the Armed Forces Radio station a speech made by President Johnson in Omaha. That speech was without a doubt the best he's ever made in his career. We were all especially glad to hear it. We almost wish this were an all-out war so that we'd know we're doing some good, but the way it is we really aren't sure what's happening.

Two nights ago we were alerted about midnight for a possible mortar attack. Nothing happened, though. Almost every night you can hear artillery and mortars all around us. The sound from the jets at the air base is also deafening. Then if you look off to the north you can hear helicopters flying around and see them spraying the area from the air with machine-gun fire, occasionally dropping a flare to light up the area. Action all around us, yet we lead practically a garrison life here, just preparing to move out.

The Vietnamese [military] also has some of its air force here. I really like their planes. They're using WWII single-engine fighter bombers. I'd much rather see them fly than all our jets, although I wouldn't trust them.

Yesterday about a half mile off to our west the Vietnamese and American air forces put on a bombing demonstration for Premier Ky. They were dropping 500 lb. bombs and napalm. It was really quite a show. Then later on yesterday we were told by an army doctor that during the demonstration one of the 500 lb. bombs fell short of the target and fell into a little village. The hospitals here are full with little kids, etc. as a result. Something like that is really too bad, especially since it was just a darn demonstration.

Dear Frances,                                                    5 July 66
In this letter I'm including some Vietnamese money. Money is "dong" in Vietnamese I guess, but they're also called piasters (French word): 200 Ps is worth a little less than two American dollars. I'm also sending you some military scrip [military payment certificates]. This is money just like and the same value of dollar bills, fives, coins, etc., however, we spend it in place of the American money. You see, when we first got here we had to turn in all our American money, and in return we got the same value in

military scrip. The reason for this is the black market. If we had American dollars here we could probably sell them for 10 times their value, so to prevent this and thus prevent the Vietnamese economy from being ruined we just don't get dollars; instead we get scrip.

This morning Capt. Eure, Roy, Harold, and myself went to Baria [actually the IATF base camp at Nui Dat] by helicopter to make arrangements. I briefly saw the place and then went on to Vung Tau with a major to check our supply system. Vung Tau and our position is the difference between night and day. Vung Tau is a resort town, still dirty though, and our position is in the middle of a jungle that's just been cleared enough for us to set up. To our front about 9,000 meters is a big jungle-covered mountain [a mountain mass called the Nui Dinh hills], and all around us is jungle occasionally cleared for rice paddies. Also, streams and rivers wind all through the area. From the air it's the most beautiful sight I've ever seen, but on the ground it's nothing but hot, wet, and mosquitoes. Our position is next to an Aussie 105-mm how. btry on our right, and the whole Aussie task force to our rear. Our left and front (west and south) face toward open territory.

Looks like we've got our work cut out for us in the coming days and months. We are supposed to leave here sometime next week by truck convoy to Baria. The highway [Highway 15] is not secure, however, we're taking it anyway. It also appears that Roy and I (the FOs) will be FOing from both the air and the ground, probably mostly ground. That's a tough break. The problem is, you see, there's no airstrip in our area, and until one is built no planes can get in, only copters. FOing from the air is generally done from small planes.

Tonight is the Fourth of July in the U.S. Guess you're all getting ready for the big night of celebrating. Last Fourth we were at your [parents'] place, weren't we? It all seems so long ago.

8 July 66

It's been a couple of days since I've last written you, and I feel bad about it. I've been running around Bien Hoa trying to get our big move coordinated, without much luck. It seems that better than half of our vehicles are still at Cam Ranh Bay, one of our first Vietnam port stops, and won't get to us until the last part of July. Maybe if we're lucky we'll be in operation about the 1st of August.

Our btry is getting one more officer, a 1/lt. to be fire direction officer. We now have a total of six officers in the btry. Ordinarily, of course, we'd only have three officers, but Chuck will be acting as a liaison officer with the Aussies, Roy and I FOS and part-time fire direction officers, and Harold XO, and of course the BC.

9 July 66

The [Vietnamese] women here take jobs just like the men, filling sandbags, etc. Of course none of them, men or women, work very hard. I think two Americans could probably do the work of 10 men or 15 women (Vietnamese) in a day; however, this way we keep them happy and ourselves from working too hard.

Let me tell you more about the town of Bien Hoa. Apparently the town was mainly under French influence a few years ago. The people still drive some French cars, and a lot of the buildings are of French design. You can still see some of the old French plantation mansions.

It's now been 45 min. since I wrote that last sentence. We just had some excitement. A grenade exploded to our rear and was returned by rifle fire from the Hawk missile unit to our west. Naturally the lights went out, and everyone started heading for the foxholes. All's clear now, and we've got a small lantern going and our tent flaps closed so no light can get out. We never did get in our foxholes, because nothing more happened. Everyone just sort of milled around for a moment and then went back to their dark tents. One of the lts. started walking our rear area with a loaded rifle; we promptly chewed his butt. He got mad and went back to his tent. A man like that will just get someone killed.

It's not been too warm here, but the humidity is so darn high. Actually we're in the cool season now. From about Jan. through April is the real hot season. Lately it hasn't rained too much. For a while it rained buckets every day, but since last week we've had only a couple of showers. At night here it gets pretty chilly sometimes.

The living conditions here are not good, but then we don't seem to mind. There are four officers living in a 12 ft. diameter hexagon tent. Our floor is dirt (sandy); we sleep on canvas cots on top of which we lay our air mattress and over that our mosquito net. All around our tent we have lumber piles, barbed wire in stacks, and also stacks of sandbags. When it rains everything is mud, including our tent floor sometimes. We're lucky in that we can take showers every day. We have a large airplane fuel tank up on wooden legs with showerheads fixed into the bottom of the tank. We really live like kings. (Ha!)

We've been getting three hot meals a day every day, so we're not starving. The food is not too good, though. This is one advantage of being in the arty. Since we don't have to move so much we have a chance to set up our mess section, and thus we get three square meals a day. The inf. on the other hand doesn't have it this good. As an arty man I'll never see the real blood and guts war of the infantry, unless of course I have to be a ground FO all the time. The btry's most dangerous mission during the year will probably be this move from here to Baria. If we don't get ambushed the btry should have it made, with the exception of course of sniper fire and an occasional mortar attack. Of course we FOS will always lead a little bit more dangerous life, but that's expected.

Yesterday afternoon the 2/35 Arty fired its first round of ammunition. Higher headquarters figured that since we'd be sitting here for a couple of weeks yet we might as well shoot. It was a real thrill. Colonels and a general were here to see our first round on its way. Then we fired all last night, as we will every night from now on while we're here. That's the way it will work here; we'll fire somewhat during the days when needed, but every night we'll shoot. Sleep comes hard with all that noise and shaking ground.

Dear Folks,                                          13 July 66
Seems like a while since I've written you all. There's not much to tell you because we're not really doing too much except trying to arrange for our move. This is really becoming a problem. A new unit over here really has problems, the big one being logistics. We can't get our equipment because transportation of such can't be gotten. I don't know what's going to happen when more troops pour in. It's all pretty discouraging. We're here but can't really do what we're supposed to do.

They did put us to work shooting from here somewhat. Every night we fire with what guns we have at suspect enemy locations. These fires are all prearranged as to location and times, so no FOS are needed. Over here about 75% or more of our firing will be of this type. They're called H&I fires, harassing and interdiction fires.

Firing artillery here is discouraging. Before you can fire, regardless of the situation, you have to be given permission from higher HQ. It should only take about a minute to fire the first round after the fire mission is received, but here it takes 10 minutes because you have to get permission [clearance].

It's raining today. Our tent floor is dirt usually, but today it's mud. Even though we've got it ditched, the water still comes in. Our tent even leaks a little. We really live in a paradise don't we? Actually we're pretty well off. The poor infantry out on operations in this weather really has it tough.

Dear sweet Frances,                                              13 July 66

Your letters today were certainly welcome. We haven't gotten any mail here the last few days. I don't know what the holdup was, but there sure were a lot of people disappointed.

We get a lot of news here. The *Stars and Stripes* newspaper (daily) covers pretty much what's happening, even the riots in Omaha, believe it or not. They even give the Omaha temperature, among other cities in the States. In addition to this we get the Armed Services Radio station from Saigon. They run the station just like those in the States, with air force or army personnel acting as disk jockeys. It's real good; of course the news is pretty much geared to happenings over here. Actually, we're a lot better informed here about the war just through news than you are in the States.

It's been raining all day today, and here it is 7:30 P.M. and even raining harder. Our tent is leaking like a sieve. It's times like this when living gets a little bit miserable. As I'm writing you I'm getting wet.

16 July 66, 1:35 A.M.

Tonight will be a long one. I'm operations officer tonight coordinating harassing and interdiction arty fires for our bn. Every night we fire all night long at possible enemy locations. Guess I might as well get used to this, because we'll be firing at night the whole year, and of course that means working on night shifts in operations and FDC. Sometimes I'll be on at night and other times during the day. I'll be on duty this morning until 6:00 A.M. Hope I can get some sleep then. I don't know if I will, though; I may go to Baria with Capt. Eure.

Today we also went to Baria and then hopped down to Vung

Tau. We're still trying to coordinate our btry movement. So far we've run into quite a few obstacles. It won't be too long anymore, though. Today we got almost all of the rest of our vehicles in. Hopefully that means we'll move down there in the next couple of days.

Today when we flew down to Baria we flew treetop level all the way in a Huey helicopter. This is the type of helicopter (chopper) you see on the news all the time, I'm sure. You can tell by the machine guns sticking out of the open doors on the sides. If you see this, chances are it's a Huey. I really like flying in one at treetop level. It's all quite exciting.

Sun. 17 July 66, 12 noon

Here it is Sun., but just another work day for me. I missed church this morning because I was out on an errand for Capt. Eure.

Just found out some stuff on R&R, so I thought I'd sit right down and tell you about it. As of now Hawaii is not an approved R&R area. It may be in the future, but I don't think we can plan on it. The next best spot is Japan. I put down for R&R during the month of Dec. in Japan. Each week the btry will be sent down a quota of so many men it can have on R&R that particular week. The btry cmdr. then determines who is to go that week by picking from the people who listed that particular month for their R&R. Do you want to fly to Japan? It looks like the only way we'll get together.

Dear Folks,                                                18 July 66

We're finally moving; things are beginning to get hectic. We're trying to take as much lumber, etc. with us as we can, but we just don't have the trucks to haul it. Not only that, but there's some politics involved in this business of being with the Aussies. The word has been put out to us that we can't live any better than they do. For example, they're living like pigs, in the mud, no shower facilities, etc. etc. Well we have access to lumber and concrete for building livable buildings at our position, but higher headquarters won't let us have any of these building materials because then we'd be living better than the Aussies. Well our btry cmdr. doesn't buy this. We will build decent quarters regardless. I suppose though that the first time a general comes to visit us the BC will be in trouble.

Dear Frances,                                          18 July 66, 8:45 P.M.

I no more than wrote *Dear Frances* to this letter and we got a fire mission. It's now 10:40 P.M. a VC squad was spotted by the infantry about 2½ miles away, and they called for fire. We gave it to them. Hopefully we got our first VC. A Btry had the shift tonight on the guns, so we have the honor of firing the first real fire mission called in by an FO for the 2/35th. All this other firing we've been doing the last week or so was merely preplotted suspect enemy locations designated to be fired at such and such a time, but tonight it was a real live fire mission where the FO thought he saw something and called in fire near his position. It's thrilling back here, but 2½ miles away I imagine the infantry had some fearsome moments.

The other btrys that moved to their areas [at Xuan Loc] were hit by a VC mortar attack last night. The btrys don't have their guns down there yet, however, the mortar shells landed at spots within the btry perimeter where the guns would ordinarily be. I imagine from now on they'll be hit off and on.

As it stands, we're still supposed to leave here this week, although our move has been delayed one day now. By Sun. we should be down there.

Wed. 20 July 66, 4:30 A.M.

Here I am again on night shift. Just came on a half hour ago, and I'll get off at 6:00 A.M., which isn't so bad; however, that still only makes five hours of sleep last night. Would have gotten to bed earlier except we stayed up shooting the bull with an Aussie lt. that happened to be in the area. They are quite the people. They talk and act like the British. Their army is practically the same as the British army; however, as you might know, they don't want to be known as being so close to the British.

Life in the staging area at Bien Hoa was boring and frustrating, but probably a good way of gradually getting adjusted to Vietnam. I guess the thing that impressed me most was the contrast—War Zone D to the north, and then the way we and other Americans around us lived in base camp conditions.

Armed Forces Radio and TV were a wonder. Never had it occurred to me that such things could exist in a combat zone. Each morning Armed Forces Radio would open its program day with the announcer's calling out, "Good morning, Vietnam." The funny thing was that as the year progressed the "good" got more drawn out. Later on it was more like, "Goo—d morning Vietnam." The "good" part sometimes seemed to last a full 30 seconds. I don't know of anyone who didn't both love and hate that method of beginning the program day. Armed Forces TV was another marvel. If you had a TV set, and we had one, owing to Captain Eure's foresight, you could watch many TV programs that were being shown Stateside (our generators supplied electric power). One night while watching "Combat," a TV series about a World War II infantry squad fighting in the European Theater, we received a fire mission. What a strange war!

The staging area food was better than we expected, but looking back on it now, it was pretty bad. At first everything was B rations. We ate an awful lot of powdered eggs, and sausage that didn't even seem like meat. The milk was terrible. Though it came in cartons and was cooled, it was reconstituted. I considered it undrinkable. It was frustrating just to go to the mess tent at mealtime. Often it was raining as we trooped past the kitchen getting our mess kits filled. We'd slog, slip, and slide through the mess line, water would drip into our food, and then we'd walk through more mud to the eating area.

The troops always seemed to have something going. One group started a Bible study program in which the members would spend hours discussing the Bible and their salvation. In contrast, some of the troops got all dressed up in full field gear including flak vest and rifle and had their buddies take pictures of them. I guess those pictures probably impressed people back home. Once we moved into our operational area, however, I never saw anyone do this again.

One of our sergeants made a big thing of showing everyone in the battery photographs of his wounded brother, who had been with the 1st Cavalry Division (Airmobile). Someone had taken pictures of the wounds: I just couldn't believe he would go around showing off those photos. His brother had been shot up pretty badly; the exit wounds in his back were holes the size of baseballs.

One of the high points of our stay at Bien Hoa was building and using our first shower. Never did I realize that something as simple as a shower could be so exciting and wonderful. Initiating it was even better: the men grabbed Captain Eure and threw him in, clothes and all.

Almost from the beginning VD became a problem for us. On our first or second day at Bien Hoa one of our cooks turned up missing. Captain Eure and I took a jeep and began driving the roads between our area and the main part of town, and sure enough, on a long portion of unguarded road there he was, heading back toward our staging area. Eure all but scared him to death with threats, but the damage was done. He was among the first to get a good dose of the clap.

While staging at Bien Hoa the 173d Airborne Brigade let us use their officers' club. We officers thought it was a good deal, but we soon got the feeling that they resented us, especially our newness. They always seemed willing to tell us real horror stories. For example, one night they told how a sergeant with three days left "in country" had thrown a hand grenade and a bad detonator had caused it to explode just as it left his hand. Not a pretty story for us with 11 months left and still no combat experience.

The time finally did come for A Battery to move, on 21 July. We loaded the trucks, cleaned our rifles and other weapons, sand-bagged the floors of the vehicles against road mines, put the windshields down, and stacked more sandbags on top of the windshields. After what seemed like an eternity of preparing and waiting, we finally made the move to our operational area base camp, with the 1st Australian Task Force at Nui Dat, just a few miles north of Baria and shown as Phuoc Le on our maps.

## 3. BASE CAMP AND
## AERIAL OBSERVATION

Dearest Frances,                              Mon. 25 July 66

I haven't written now for four days. Please forgive me, but there has just not been an opportunity until now. Last Fri. we convoyed from Bien Hoa to here [Nui Dat]. It was a pretty hairy convoy, and we were expecting to be ambushed by a VC battalion. Luckily for us, not a thing happened. I was leading one portion (serial of about 15 trucks) of the convoy consisting of only cargo trucks and no heavy weapons. Lt. Heindrichs was leading a similar column, and the rest of the officers had columns of trucks protected by our guns.

Today our listening post outside the perimeter received sniper fire, but no one was hurt. Not too far away a big battle [the major action of Operation Hobart] is raging, and it keeps us jumping. Believe me, this area is not quite as secure as Bien Hoa.

In a few days myself, Roy, and our FO sections will move out of the btry and move in with the Australian infantry. Here we'll train and get used to their system and then go out with them on operations. Roy and I will be both ground and air FOs. Since we'll be with the Australians, we'll dress like them, in their fatigues, [use] their weapons, and [wear] their hats. They don't wear helmets like we do; they just wear a floppy old hat.

We don't get mail here very often. I'll probably get your mail about twice a week, and I'll be able to send mail about that much.

We killed a cobra snake here the other day and several tarantulas. Real nice place we've got here.

The Australians and New Zealanders are really fine people to work with. All lights here go out at 7:30 P.M. From then on it's complete blackout and no movement in our area or any area.

Today I went out on my first patrol. Actually it wasn't a patrol, it was a reaction force to counter some Vietnamese we saw about 1,000 meters in front of our perimeter. I didn't have to go along, but I thought I'd go just to see what it would be like. Well, we went out through rice paddies, water, mud, tall grass, and thick jungle and didn't see anything. Then all of a sudden we heard Vietnamese talking in the brush. We charged through the brush (I cut my arm up a bit on fishhook thorns) and into a clearing. Lo and behold, what did we run into but a Vietnamese group of children herding water buffalo. Well, we were all quite relieved because we thought they might be vc.

It's really kind of a poor situation for the civilians here. All farmland [rice paddies] and jungle to the front of us, the New Zealanders and Aussies have declared off limits to Vietnamese civilians. Any that come into this area we may shoot. Well, the civilians keep coming here because it's their land. Essentially we've just said "get off your land or we'll shoot you." Of course if we didn't do this, we'd probably have more vc in the area than we have already; however, there are lots of innocent people getting hurt. For example, yesterday myself, Roy, and the bc were on an op looking for practice targets to shoot at when suddenly we saw some real live tgts. to shoot at. Well, we called arty fire on them, really only meaning to scare them because we thought they might be farmers. As luck would have it, the fire landed right on top of them. People ran all which way; however, the cattle they were herding were all killed. We killed some poor farmers' most valuable possession. Of course, for all we know they may have been vc by night, but still it makes a person feel kind of bad.

Dear Folks,                                              29 July 66
Sorry I haven't written for so long, but in our new position we are definitely fighting a war as compared to being in Bien Hoa. Bien Hoa was like a Stateside camp compared to this.

Here it's really muddy and dirty. None of us have been dry and clean for over a week now. I haven't had a bath since we've been here. The darn scorpions and snakes are thick here too. It rains about three-fourths of every 24 hrs., and the rest of the time it's extremely hot. The food is good, however. We brought a food freezer with us and thus can keep fresh food all the time. There's only one drawback to this, though: we have to make an armed convoy into Vung Tau every day to pick up food. I guess it's worth the chance, though. I led our first two convoys to Vung Tau the beginning of this week. We had no action on either one of my convoys, thank goodness!

Tonight the other FO, Roy Minick, was rushed off to the Aussie infantry [5th Battalion, Royal Australian Regiment (5RAR)] to go out on an operation sometime in the future. I guess I'll be doing the same in the few weeks; however, for the next week or so I'll be flying air missions for the Aussie task force out of Vung Tau. I've already flown two missions, one yesterday and one last Fri. Yesterday I adjusted [artillery] fire from my helicopter on a hill [Nui Nghe] near us. We have been using the hill as a registration point (we fire, and as a result of firings we can apply special corrections to the guns to make up for variations in air temp, etc.), the hill we thought being fairly safe and clear. Well today another helicopter flew in the same area and the VC opened up on him with heavy automatic weapons. Guess that's just the way war goes.

Myself and my FO section are being assigned to a New Zealand battery of arty [161 Battery, Royal New Zealand Artillery (RNZA)], and from there we'll go out on operations with the Aussies. As a result of our btry being assigned to the Aussie task force, we have to follow their procedures. For example, their radio procedure and arty fire mission procedures are different than ours, so we have to learn their way and do it that way. I suppose about the time I learn their methods I'll be transferred to another btry in the bn and have to relearn American procedure again.

As a whole so far, the Aussies and New Zealand officers seem much better than ours. They're all so darn professional. They really impress me.

Last night we had a VC probe against us. My recon. sgt. took a shot at one at a range of about 20 yds. in the dark and missed. We called in arty and mortar fire. Eventually at about 2:00 A.M. things calmed down and we all sacked out.

Happy birthday, Dad. Hope you had a good one. I imagine you had company and made homemade ice cream. Ice cream sure would taste good about now. Speaking of ice cream, I sure do miss drinking milk. I haven't had real milk since I boarded the plane at Colo. Springs. All the milk from then on has been canned or re-constituted. I just can't stand to drink that except in coffee.

Well, I'd better close for now. Will write again when I can. It will probably be sometime next week. I haven't even been able to write Frances more than two letters since we've gotten here be-cause as soon as it gets dark we just don't have lights. We're under a strict blackout. So if I can't work my writing in during the day I just can't write unless I'm on night duty in the FDC.

Life in our new base camp at Nui Dat was just plain dirty and uncomfortable during the early days of our occupation. Since we spent considerable time building bunkers and digging mortar pits, the red mud of the area covered our boots and clothing, dye-ing them a deep reddish brown. Even our skin began to absorb this red mud, and after a while, since we had no showers at first, it was hard to tell whether a man was tanned, muddy, or both. Even the letters I wrote home were smudged with the red mud of Nui Dat.

During the day we directed most of our attention toward secur-ing our perimeter, building personnel bunkers, and shooting fire missions that came in occasionally. We found that building with sandbags filled with mud required some proficiency. You couldn't just stack them; rather, you laid them a row at a time like bricks, beat them flat with a board, and then laid another row, beating them flat the same way.

Every morning before first light we observed what the Aussies called "stand to," and then at last light we observed "stand down." It was a solemn ritual, each of us positioned at our assigned posts on the perimeter or elsewhere in the battery area, all of us armed, weapons ready, peering out across the barbed wire and paddy toward the jungle. In theory we were watching for an enemy at-tack, unlikely as it was during these hours. Charlie wasn't that pre-dictable. It seemed to me that the Aussies were really just hanging on to an old military custom of years gone by. Whatever the basis, however, it did get everyone up, awake, and functional at dawn and ended the day in the same manner.

By Australian Task Force policy, "stand down" was also the sig-nal to roll down our shirt sleeves, or to put our shirts back on. The mosquitoes didn't bother us during the day, but at night they were a problem. The possibility of getting killed by the VC was bad enough; no one was fool enough to give malaria a chance as well. We were especially sensitive to the threat because several Australians had already died from a rather severe strain, so we were told.

Soon after our arrival, the New Zealanders assigned a full-time liaison officer to work with us in learning task force artillery procedures. Our Kiwi first lieutenant turned out to be a true professional and a tremendous asset to us in learning the New Zealand / Australian radio and artillery system. Although we continued to use our own technical procedures, we had to adjust our communications to mesh with the Aussie/Kiwi system. After all, the Australian artillery regimental commander was our direct boss, so we had to conform. This was a blessing in disguise, because a few months later all U.S. and NATO forces around the world converted to a standard artillery communication system based on the British model, which was in fact the Aussie/Kiwi system we were already using.

During these early days in base camp and during the entire year thereafter when the battery wasn't out on operation, we made regular supply runs to Vung Tau, 25 miles south, to pick up food, ammunition, and supplies in general. In addition to supplies, our convoys brought back news of what was happening elsewhere "in country" and in Vung Tau itself. One supply convoy came back with the startling news that the quartermaster battalion we had been with on board the troopship had suffered several KIAS (killed in action) in Vung Tau. Vung Tau? Vung Tau, an in country R&R center, was one of the most secure places in Vietnam. What had happened was that several men of the quartermaster unit had gotten involved with some local Vietnamese bar girls in Vung Tau. The girls' Vietnamese boyfriends, ARVN (Army of the Republic of Vietnam) soldiers, rather upset over the whole situation, had tossed grenades into the bar where the GIS and the girls were drinking, killing several. What a way to die for your country! I've often wondered what their commanding officer wrote to their families. I would bet the letters said they had died while performing their mission against the Communist insurgents in defense of South Vietnam. I wonder how many of our KIAS in Vietnam, and in other wars for that matter, occurred in similar unhappy circumstances.

We established one of the biggest luxuries of base camp life early during our stay. Our carpenters constructed a couple of one-

and two-hole outdoor toilets, "shitters" as we called them. They really were rather attractive and, in the best tradition of years gone by, included side vents and a roof. Beneath the seats, as waste receptacles, we put 50-gallon drums that had been cut in half and half filled with diesel fuel. Then, for sanitation, every morning the first sergeant detailed one man to burn the contents, an honest-to-goodness "shit detail"!

My duties at base camp were short-lived because of upcoming aerial observation duties. But during those first days I led convoys to Vung Tau, pulled shifts in the battery Fire Direction Center, and helped build bunkers. By the end of the first weeks of work we had the battery base camp area in fairly good shape. Gun emplacements were well on the way to being sandbagged, and we had started working on our sleeping tents as well. We were building three- to four-foot-high sandbag walls around each tent, high enough so we were protected from mortar shrapnel as we slept, unless of course a round landed directly inside. The initial hard work was done, but the battery continued to make improvements during the entire year when not on operation. As for me, it was time to begin seeing the war firsthand.

Dearest Frances,                                    2 August 66

This week, as I believe I said earlier, I'm air observer for the task force area. I make two two-hour combat recons. daily and two courier runs daily, which amounts to about five hrs. flying time per day. By the end of tomorrow I will have earned my wings [Aircraft Crewman Badge]. I don't mind the flying at all; however, I'd rather fly by copter than plane.

Just heard some real good news over the radio. Hawaii is now an approved R&R spot. I'm changing my request immediately from Japan to Hawaii. Good-bye for now, darling. Just pray that I can meet you there.

3 August 66

Since I've been flying, I haven't had anything to do when I get back to the btry. I think I've told you, but here's the way it works. I leave here at 5:30 P.M. by copter for Vung Tau, hop on a plane there, fly for two hrs., and then go back to Vung Tau, spend the night there, get up at 4:45 A.M. the next morning, fly by plane until 8:00 A.M., take a copter back here to the btry, and then the whole cycle begins again at 5:30 P.M. I fly about four to five hrs. a day.

Staying in Vung Tau with the Aussie army aviation outfit is nice. They have a club and very good food. They remind me of people on *Twelve O'Clock High* [a 1960s TV series based on the World War II bomber offensive over Europe].

Last night I got shot at for the first time over here. I was up flying, we were just about to head back to Vung Tau at about 8:00 P.M. (had been flying the last two hrs.) when we decided to take a look at a spot one more time. We looked, didn't see anything, so we turned on our flying lights and headed for home. Just as soon as those lights went on a machine gun opened up. The pilot went into a wild loop to avoid being hit. We shut those lights off promptly and headed for Vung Tau. You know, honey, I wasn't even too scared.

5 August 66, 0800 A.M.

Just got finished with my morning flight. The pilot just dropped me off at a little airfield. I'm standing here waiting for a copter to pick me up and take me back to the btry. We did this yesterday morning too. I don't particularly like this, because I'm out in the middle of nowhere, all by myself, just waiting. It kind of gives you the creeps, especially since there's a Vietnamese army outpost here. They're supposed to be friendly, but of course some are VC. Believe me, I'm standing here with my submachine gun loaded and ready. I'll finish the letter when I get back to the btry, OK? Here comes the copter now.

6 August 66

I've been getting mail from you almost every day now. I sure am sorry you didn't get any from me for a week. I've been writing again almost every day, so you should be getting more mail pretty soon. Just don't worry, honey, I'm all right.

By tomorrow at this time I'll have 35 hrs. of flight time and about 30 missions. Roy was supposed to fly next week, but he's going on an operation with the infantry, so I'll be flying again next week, which means at this time next week I'll have about 60 missions in and 70 hours. About the middle of the month I go out on operation with the infantry. This month will go by pretty fast since I'll be so busy.

9 August 66

I'm writing tonight from Vung Tau, where the unit I'm flying with is located. This unit, by the way, is an Australian unit, 161

Recce [Reconnaisance] Flight of the Army Aviation Corps. I wish so much this was a permanent arrangement. I really like these people. In our area where the infantry and artillery men are located relations seem to be a little cooler, but here they're all just like a bunch of college buddies, almost. The crazy fools sure do like to drink. One night, in fact, the commanding officer here ordered me to stay at the bar and drink. Of course I didn't mind at the time, but was I in bad shape the next day.

I have practically zero time now for myself. I get up at 4:45 A.M., fly till about 8:00, and get back to Baria [Nui Dat] by 8:30. Then from 8:30 till 9:30 I'm debriefed. At 10:00 I have to be at the New Zealand artillery btry for training all day long until 4:00 P.M. Then at 4:30 P.M. I leave once again for Vung Tau to catch my flight. Believe me, it's hectic.

Dear Folks,                                                    12 August 66

Day after tomorrow I'm moving with my FO section to the 6th Bn, Royal Australian Regiment [6RAR] (Infantry). We will live there almost permanently. When they go out, we go out. This could prove to be quite interesting.

We finally got a shower in here and a couple of concrete floors. Our food is fresh and very good. The biggest problem is the rain, mud, and our living quarters. Our whole area is mud constantly. We really get rain here.

We've had a couple of USO shows come in here lately. So far no American stars, though. All we've had so far is Australian and Korean. They break the monotony, though.

Dearest Frances,                                              14 August 66

Tonight I'm in the btry area for a change. I finished my flying this morning and now I go to the infantry. This morning was rather exciting. I was flying [very low] over some Aussie inf. when they flushed two VC out of the brush into a rice paddy. They shot one out in the middle of a paddy and the other as he dove for cover. They sent four men out into the paddy after the one they had knocked down. They ran up to him (about within 10 ft.), and all four opened up with submachine guns and just blew that poor VC to shreds. It seemed like murder seeing as how the poor guy was already down, but I guess that's war. The other VC they captured alive. I never thought I'd see a man killed quite like that. I guess we don't take prisoners any more than they do, really. The sad part of it was, the supposed vc were not carrying weapons, or at least when they were shot they weren't. For all anyone knows, they may have been just two scared farmers.

Flying as an aerial observer seemed like the first important job I'd had in Vietnam. The previous jobs—convoy commander, pulling shifts in the Fire Direction Center, and building bunkers—were all necessary but didn't leave any feeling of really contributing to the war effort. Flying as task force air observer was important to everyone in that it provided the Australians with aerial intelligence for their entire area of operation.

Living and flying with the men of 161 Recce Flight was an experience to be long remembered. Their base camp on the sandy beaches of Vung Tau was a far cry from the red mud of Nui Dat. The tents and other facilities were the same; the difference was the ground they stood on. Whereas Nui Dat was a constant quagmire of red mud and water, the 161 Reece Flight base camp lay sprawled over the dunes of an ocean beach. The sand was clean, warm in the day and cool at night. Furthermore, mosquitoes were minimal, snakes absent, and other bugs and nuisances unnoticeable. It was a real paradise compared with the mud, water, banana trees, paddies, rubber-tree groves, grass, jungle, and insects of the task force area 25 miles to the north.

The pilots themselves were very different from the Australians I'd previously had contact with. They were uninhibited, fun-loving, and generally a happy lot compared with the Australian and New Zealand artillery officers I'd met at Nui Dat. Of course, I hadn't yet met the infantry officers. Each of the three fixed-wing pilots I flew with had his own variety of experiences, but as a whole they were carefree and seemed oblivious to the danger they faced daily during observation missions. I felt ashamed of myself for worrying so much in contrast to all the fun they seemed to be having. Perhaps they worried too, but if they did it certainly wasn't apparent. Looking back, however, I don't think I ever expressed my worries and fears to anyone, and I probably put up as good a front as any of them. Such is the role men play in war.

The oldest of the three spotter plane pilots had the dubious distinction of frequently getting shot at. Few other 161 Recce pilots had this problem to any great extent. And, the one time I was shot at during my two weeks of flying, I was with him. Of the other two fixed-wing pilots, one was very young, a lieutenant and a real hot-rodder, who continually tried to scare the living daylights out of me. The other was also a lieutenant, tall, slim, and a bit effeminate. Both were the very best of pilots, the latter the best map reader from the air that I'd ever seen and also extremely competent at reacting fast in a life-or-death situation. I knew from personal experience.

The life-or-death situation occurred while we were flying 9,000 meters west of the task force base camp area over the Nui Dinh hills. The hills rose about 2,000 feet above the flatlands, and from them you could see most of Phuoc Tuy Province. We flew these hills almost daily, figuring that the vc must be using them as observation points for scanning our base camp area. We had been flying low (under 100 feet sometimes) down in the valleys, along the mountainsides, and skimming the peaks. Suddenly my pilot said something about cross-drafts and air pockets. He took us up immediately, but before reaching a safe height we hit an air pocket and dropped considerably before stabilizing. Had we not begun climbing just before hitting the air pocket, we would probably have ended up plastered on the side of one of the Nui Dinh hills, either dead or injured and over 9,000 meters from any friendly help. My pilot shrugged it off as just another incident, the kind that I guess was commonplace to him. As for me, my stomach practically had to be scraped off the cockpit ceiling. I say that figuratively, however. Not once did I lose my cookies while flying with 161 Recce Flight.

The fixed-wing aircraft we flew were not the o1 Bird Dogs used by U.S. Army pilots and observers. They were small single-engine, four-passenger Cessnas, wider than the Bird Dogs. In the Aussie Cessna the observer sat next to the pilot, and there was room in the backseat to toss extra maps, weapons, and equipment. The U.S. Bird Dog was a two-seater with the observer directly behind the pilot. The backseat observer in the Bird Dog had no access to the aircraft controls except for a second "stick" folded down onto the floor. In an emergency one had to reach down, raise the control stick, engage it, and pray that the aircraft could be brought under control. The Aussie Cessna had dual controls that allowed the observer to take over more easily if necessary. The only prob-

42

lem was that most observers, including me, had not been trained to fly. My pilots, however, spent some time making sure I at least knew a few fundamentals of aircraft control, and on several occasions they allowed me to half-fly the plane. Though I was partial to the Cessna, the U.S. Bird Dog allowed better observation to the sides, an advantage I thought was more than offset by being up front with the pilot in the Cessna.

During the four hours or more a day of flying by fixed-wing aircraft, our mission was simply to look over the Australian area of operations for signs of activity, record its type and location, and engage targets of opportunity with artillery fire. We spent most of our time observing and recording traffic on the roads, cart tracks on trails and across fields, freshly dug earth, bunker sites, and so on. During my last days of flying, 13 and 14 August, we noticed an exceptional number of cart tracks and more civilians than usual on the roads. Significantly, a few days later mortar fire struck our task force base camp, and soon after came the battle of Long Tan.

I didn't call in artillery fire often. Other than registering an artillery battery one day, no one particular fire mission stands out in my mind. I do recall clearly, however, a fire mission *not* called in. We were again flying the Nui Dinh hills and happened on a little stone house near the peak of one of the mountains. We flew past it several times but saw nothing. Then, on a final run, I chanced to look back after we had passed it and saw a man come out of the house and watch us fly away. It would have been proper for me to call in a fire mission because the hills were in a "free fire zone," designated areas where the only humans were assumed to be VC. Any person, armed or not, within a free fire zone could legitimately be engaged and killed. Well, the man wasn't armed and he hadn't shot at us, so I decided to let him go. Mistake or not, I couldn't see blowing him away when he hadn't threatened us. At the time I speculated that he was either a VC observer or just an innocent Vietnamese civilian living on the mountain. One month later, in September, I climbed that mountain with the infantry and got involved in several small firefights, mostly with VC administrative organizations and their protective infantrymen.

During my two weeks with 161 Recce Flight, the ground crews equipped our Cessnas with wing-mounted rocket launchers. They hadn't had these before, and the addition made the pilots feel aggressive. There were no rocket sights on the planes, so each of my pilots made grease-pencil marks on the windshield so all he had to do was line up the makeshift sights on the target and blaze away. I think most of the rockets were of the white phosphorous type. What a time we had with this new toy! We'd find abandoned huts in a free fire zone and dive in for the kill. Once in a while we'd even hit the target. Primarily, however, we were to use the rockets to mark target areas for artillery and air strikes. If one was in the area, you could even call in a "Spooky" (also called a dragon ship, or "Puff the Magic Dragon"), an old C-47 air force plane equipped with high rate of fire miniguns. Spooky, with its tremendous firepower, could saturate an area with bullets. I once observed Spooky operate at night and saw the spray of tracers from its guns rise and fall like water from a high-pressure hose. At any rate, the rockets were a welcome addition to our aircraft and broke the monotony of just flying reconnaissance.

Every day I flew from the task force base camp at Nui Dat to Vung Tau and then back with the helicopter courier. Our base camp during these days didn't have an airstrip, so the fixed-wing aircraft had no way of getting in. The 161 Recce Flight aircraft used for these courier flights were little bubble-front helicopters (Sioux), the same type (though probably a newer model) used to carry wounded to hospitals during the Korean War. In addition to picking up observers for reconnaissance flights, they ran mail, documents, and passengers to and from Vung Tau and the task force base camp every morning and afternoon.

Frankly, I enjoyed the helicopter flights more than the entire reconnaissance by fixed-wing plane. Like the fixed-wing pilots, my three pilots for these runs were carefree, cocky, young, and I think even more daredevil. All three were lieutenants: one was blond and somewhat bucktoothed, a bit older than me, married, and with a couple of small children; one was dark, single, extremely likable, and a real hell-raiser; and the third was tall, blond, blue-eyed, cool and calm, the son of a World War II German panzer division officer. The last was so aloof I never did get to know him, but I drank with the other two night after night in the officers' mess, and we generally carried on a relationship as if we were fraternity brothers. A few days after my flying ended, one of them earned a citation for bravery in the battle of Long Tan. The other made a crash landing some time later but survived.

During the courier runs, we did much more than just fly a straight path to and from Vung Tau. The pilots were constantly honing their skills, so most of the time we flew 10 to 20 feet off the ground, above paddies, in and out of clearings, over and under telephone wires, along the jungle edge, and then up over the tree-tops with a flick of the control stick. On occasion we would look for snipers that had taken potshots at the helicopters from abandoned huts hours or maybe days before. We would dive at the huts or come in low, and I would hang out the open side door with Owen submachine gun and grenade at hand, ready to deal out due reward to our enemy. There was no fear. It was just a game, the two of us laughing and talking over the helicopter intercom.

On one occasion practice all but scared me to death. We were flying our little bubble-front chopper high, at about 1,500 feet, just south of the base camp. The pilot was letting me fly, turn, and then recover. As soon as I had finished and he had control again, he switched off the engine and we began a powerless dive toward an abandoned concrete airstrip near a South Vietnamese army outpost. We hit the deck at a rather steep angle and, to my surprise, skidded to a rough but safe landing. Only then did he explain that we had practiced an emergency autorotation landing. Autorotation, as he explained, was a method whereby helicopters could land without power if the rotor blades could be kept at the correct angle, maintaining a certain level of powerless revolution. The descent, though fast, was usually not fatal, I was told. We practiced this many times thereafter, though I never really appreciated its value until later when I learned that one of the pilots had saved his life by autorotating to safety on a road north of the task force base camp.

On two consecutive days during the two weeks of flying, my Cessna fixed-wing aircraft landed on an old, semiabandoned airstrip south of the task force base camp and dropped me off to await pickup by the courier helicopter. Both times I protested, but both times I gave in to the argument that a South Vietnamese army outpost was nearby and would protect me should I need it. If there was an outpost near the strip it was well hidden, because I never did see it. As far as I was concerned, I was alone; and had I been threatened, I wasn't sure the Vietnamese would have helped.

For a few minutes during each of the two days, I huddled against a tin shack alongside the airstrip, hoping no vc would play games with me. It's probably fortunate that no South Vietnamese soldiers came around: I'd probably have shot them. How I managed to write a letter to Frances on one of those stopovers, I'll never know. I guess at the time I didn't realize the full danger. In fact I didn't understand how dangerous this stop really was until about December or January, when in the middle of the night we (A Battery) got a call to fire in support of the ARVN based in the town near the airstrip. On that occasion one full vc main force regiment walked into that little ARVN-held town and walked back out with a whole ARVN infantry company—people, weapons, and all. That's how safe my airstrip was!

When we weren't flying, we drank. Oh, how we drank! Living with 161 Recce Flight for two weeks of evenings and nights was almost more than I could physically endure, but I enjoyed every moment. It was an emotional release that you couldn't have at the task force base camp. Here they had electric lights in the tents, whereas when it got dark at Nui Dat that was it, at least during the early months.

After coming in from the afternoon reconnaissance at about 8:30 or 9:00, we always headed for the officers' mess, a combined club and dining tent they had fixed up with a board floor, a bar, tables, chairs, and the ever present dart board. At the mess we drank, ate, and then drank some more until midnight or later almost every night. This made it difficult to get up in the morning, but I survived for the two weeks. How they did it week after week and month after month is beyond my comprehension.

On at least one occasion during the two weeks they found some reason to really celebrate—the queen's birthday, or something. It was one toast after another, food, more drinks ("piss," as they called beer) and more and more toasting—the queen, the commander, the war, those bloody pommy bastards (the British), and so on. The most frequent toast, however, was uniquely Australian, and we drank to it again and again: "Two eyes, two hands, . . . beneath the Southern Cross I stand, so up the old red rooster and more piss."

The two weeks of flying, my most meaningful and exciting duty to date, finally and regretfully ended. Actually I was lucky, because task force observers usually flew only one week at a time, but I had

had to fly an extra week for Roy Minick. All together I had accumulated nearly 100 hours of flying time during my short stint as IATF aerial observer.

The end of these two weeks did not mean the end of my flying in Vietnam. In the months to come I made other observation flights with American pilots in the 01 Bird Dog, flew briefly now and again to register the battery, and rode the troop-carrying Huey time and again while with the infantry. The infantry! I had finally reached the juncture in my tour that I dreaded most—FOing with the infantry.

# 4. WITH THE INFANTRY: LONG TAN AND OPERATION SMITHFIELD

Dear Frances,                                    15 August 66

Today my section and I moved over to the 6th Bn Royal Australian Regiment of infanteers [infantry]. At the present we're with bn HQ, and our job will probably be somewhat administrative. As for the future, I don't know. We may go out with the infantry about the end of the month.

I'm living in a tent with one other 2/lt Aussie (married) officer. He's a real nice guy. He and his wife were married only three weeks when he left home for here in June. Actually, honey, I guess we're not so bad off. He and his wife, like us, are trying to meet each other on R&R.

Well, darling, there's just not much to write; tonight I'm almost happy. I miss you, but I'm so at ease. I know you're well taken care of, I know I'm as well cared for as is possible, and finally I know we're all being looked after by the good Lord. What more can any human look for? The only thing more is togetherness, and that too will come with time. So darling, be cheerful and happy, because I suddenly am. All in all, this is probably worthwhile.

Becoming an FO for the infantry is what I had dreaded most, but now the time had finally come. I'm not sure why Captain Eure had insisted that my section function with the Australian infantry. We really weren't needed, since 161 Battery, Royal New Zealand Artillery (RNZA), which was in direct support of 6RAR, had its full complement of four FOs serving with each of 6RAR's infantry companies, A, B, C, and D. My section and I were simply excess, as I viewed it. Irrefutably, however, battalion HQ 6RAR was our new home, and my boss was now the New Zealand battery commander, Major Harry Honner.

Being under the command of a battery commander who was a major and who lived with the infantry as Major Honner did was foreign to me. Under the New Zealand–Australian artillery system (really the British system), BCS were majors instead of captains as in the U.S. artillery. Furthermore, whereas American BCS remained at the battery and commanded it, New Zealand and Australian BCS moved in with the outfit for which their battery provided direct artillery fire support. Under this system the BC was the senior artillery adviser to the infantry battalion commander and also commanded the FOS who lived and worked with each of the infantry battalion's rifle companies. The BC did not directly supervise his battery; that duty fell to the battery 2IC (second-in-command), who remained with the battery itself.

While this different role of the BC took some getting used to during the early days of my infantry assignment, their FO system was an even greater surprise. All the FOS were captains or senior first lieutenants, the most experienced and capable officers of their batteries. Not only that, the FO assignment was sought after as "the job to have." In contrast, FOS in the American artillery were usually junior lieutenants, and the job itself was regarded as the most dangerous and least desirable of any. As I moved in with the infantry, therefore, it came as quite a shock to find that the Aussies and Kiwis assumed I must be the "chosen one" from my battery to have gotten such a coveted assignment. Mistaken as they were, moving in with the Aussies and working for a New Zealand artillery battery proved interesting and unforgettable.

Living conditions at 6RAR were vastly different than at A Battery, even though the two units lay only about 2,000 meters from each other in the base camp area. Whereas A Battery stood out in the open on the western edge of the rubber plantation that contained the 1st Australian Task Force base camp, 6RAR was spread along the eastern side and right among the trees. Whereas the A Battery area was sunny and hot, so that the monsoon rains dried quickly, the 6RAR area was dim, cooler, and always muddy. At night the difference was even more apparent. Within the A Battery area the moon or starlight made it possible to move about fairly easily, but under the rubber trees of the 6RAR area, nighttime was a black nightmare. It was impossible to see even a few inches in front of your face. The Aussies had strung white engineer tape from tent to tent so that you could get from place to place at night by blindly holding on to it. But you had better know which tape to grab, or you might follow one to someplace you didn't intend. The blackness certainly discouraged going to the latrine at night. And it was especially shocking to run head on into someone following the same tape in the opposite direction.

The latrines were especially bad. At A Battery we had our one- and two-holers, but at 6RAR latrines were simply slit trenches with seats over them. No more than 20 meters out behind my assigned tent stood the officers' latrine. It was canvas enclosed, muddy, and fly beseiged, and I absolutely hated using it. Though I've always considered defecation a time to ponder, reflect, relax, and plan, in this area it was do your duty and flee.

On the first or second day of our stay with 6RAR, they issued my FO section and me all Australian clothing and equipment (gear, as the Aussies called it). It was important for us to be indistinguishable from anyone else when we moved out into the jungle. Charlie might key on anyone who looked different, although realistically FOS and the other officers stood out because they always had a radio man close at hand. The back-mounted radio with antenna sticking up was a dead giveaway that an officer was one or two men off. Regardless of this problem, which you couldn't do anything about, the Aussies believed—and I fully agreed—that there was no sense tempting Charlie by looking different in clothing and equipment. So, except at base camp, we dressed just like them.

They issued us so much new gear on top of what we already had that I ended up storing some of my U.S. equipment back at A Battery. I got shirts, pants, boots, bush hats, backpack (an old khaki British one), air mattress, mosquito net, nylon blanket, heating tablets with small metal folding stove, water purification tablets, four water bottles (canteens), entrenching tool, machete, extra ammo pouches, 9-mm Owen submachine gun with bayonet, Owen magazines, plenty of 9-mm ammunition, compass, insect repellent, pocketknife, a short length of coiled rope, shelter halves, and a 9-mm Browning automatic pistol with holster and one extra magazine.

Most of the Aussie equipment, in my opinion, was superior to our own. The Australians were expert in jungle warfare, so their equipment was mostly jungle developed and tested. Their shelter halves, air mattress, mosquito net, and nylon blanket, for example, could be rolled into a very small bundle and easily carried in the backpack along with rations and other items. Similar U.S. gear was much bulkier. The Americans' large canvas shelter halves, heavy air mattress, and bulky mosquito net wouldn't even fit into a pack. Aussie fatigues and boots, however, were not as good as ours. Our fatigues were lightweight and specifically designed for jungle wear, with plenty of pockets, whereas theirs were of a heavy cotton similar to our conventional fatigues. Their boots, though extremely high-quality, were the high leather waterproof type and in my opinion were not well suited for areas where we were likely to step into water well above our boot tops. They were adequate for base camp duty, however. Our own boots were light, with green canvas tops, and had air vents in the leather bottoms. There was no way to keep our feet dry in them, but the water could escape and eventually, because of the vents, our feet would dry. The Aussies would trade almost anything for American jungle fatigues and boots.

Other Aussie equipment proved as much of a blessing as their lightweight sleeping gear. Their shoulder backpack was a better idea than the American-issue waist pack. The waist pack clipped directly onto the pistol belt, so in a firefight there was no way to roll over without raising your body. Furthermore, it was difficult to take off without first removing the pistol belt, to which the ammo pouches were attached. The Aussie shoulder pack, on the other hand, with two canteens and entrenching tool attached, could be tossed off when necessary, leaving us free to roll and move with only pistol belt, two canteens, first-aid packet, and ammo pouches still attached to our bodies. At any rate, their equipment and their thinking on how to use it were excellent.

My tent in the base camp area was typical of all Australian and New Zealand tents. First one tent was put up, then a larger tent was placed over it so there was a space between the two. This allowed for cooler living because the top covering either absorbed or reflected the sunlight while the air space between acted as insulation. Furthermore, it was double protection against leakage. I also had a wooden floor in my tent, which was certainly welcome in view of the damp or downright muddy conditions under the rubber trees of 6RAR's camp.

The Aussies didn't wear helmets. They didn't believe in them and long since, perhaps during World War II jungle fighting, had discarded them in favor of a little cotton or nylon bush hat. The bush hat looked like a rain hat; some men wound a length of nylon cord around the hatband, often in decorative zigzag fashion, for use in a number of ways depending on the situation. In the 5RAR (5th Battalion Royal Australian Regiment), the other 1ATF infantry battalion and our perimeter neighbor to the north, men often used pieces of cloth for identification or decoration. The vc main force units and the vc provisional battalion of our area also wore hats of this general nature, and in later years GIs in Vietnam wore them too. Maybe the Aussies knew what they were doing in discarding their helmets for these little hats, and perhaps the advantages of lightness, quiet and better hearing did indeed offset what little protection the helmets offered.

Our rations initially left much to be desired. Though I can't remember what 6RAR base camp meals consisted of during our first weeks, I clearly remember wishing I were back at A Battery chowing down on fresh A rations. Perhaps more than anything, though, the muddy and bleak conditions of 6RAR's area made almost everything seem distasteful. This all changed eventually, however. During the fall of 1966 some of the 6RAR officers constructed a beautiful (at least it seemed so then) tin structure that served as the officers' mess and bar. Only then, when we were finally able to eat at tables, did the food seem edible—in fact, excellent.

One of the things that struck me about the Aussie-Kiwi way of living was that each officer had an enlisted man assigned to him as a batman (orderly). These batmen did the laundry, cleaned the tents and weapons, cooked the rations out in the bush for their officers, and in general looked out for every little personal need. I learned that in the jungle the batman also functioned as a sort of personal bodyguard for his officer and was often in the best position to take charge if the officer was hurt or killed. Though I never did see a batman take over for an officer, some Aussies fondly described such situations from years gone by. The Aussie and Kiwi officers were constantly urging me to take on a batman for myself—to either make my radio operator one or take one of theirs. Of course I couldn't do it, nor did I believe in the idea. But as the weeks went by, especially while out on operation, I certainly began to see its advantages.

Some of the 6RAR officers I got to know during these early days in the battalion came to be among the best friends (mates, as the Aussies and Kiwis said) I'd ever had. First Lieutenant Don Parsons was among the first I met, and without a doubt he was one of the most likable and friendliest mates I had. He was in his 40s, old for a first lieutenant, but I soon discovered why. He was a World War II veteran and a veteran of other Australian involvements who had risen through the ranks to the coveted position of company sergeant major. Then for retirement purposes (higher pay) he had accepted a commission as a lieutenant—actually a comedown in terms of prestige. Don was warm, friendly, and helpful, and he knew more about the United States than I did. We spent many long nights on duty in the battalion TOC (Tactical Operations Center) during which I managed to demonstrate again and again a lack of knowledge about my own country. Equally embarrassing, I knew absolutely nothing about Australia.

I developed another warm friendship with First Lieutenant, later Captain, Les Peters. Les was the battalion 81-mm mortar platoon leader and took it upon himself to show me around and introduce me to some of the officers and men of the rifle companies. On one particular day Les took me down to C Company, where I met the company commander and the C Company mortar FO. That same day we also went over to D Company, but we saw few people because they had just left the base camp on patrol. That patrol ultimately led to many of them being killed or wounded in a battle that would go down in Australian military history as "the battle of Long Tan," a battle that was my initiation into the real war in Vietnam, only four days after joining the infantry.

The countdown for the "big battle" of the war for the Australians began during the early morning hours of Wednesday 17 August 1966, my second night with 6RAR. The night was stormy, with wind blowing and rain falling heavily. At about 3:00 A.M. my tent mate and I awakened to what we thought was extremely violent thunder and lightning. We got up off our cots, walked around a little, noticed bright flashes outside that we took for lightning, and then went back to bed. The next morning we awoke to discover that the entire task force base camp had been mortared and had taken recoilless rifle fire as well. Not far from our own area several 82-mm Chicom (a term applied to weapons manufactured in

Communist China) mortar shells had hit. Though casualties were light, the attack meant a significant VC force was very near. My tent mate and I felt like fools, having slept through the whole thing, but we figured we had fared better than most of the people in the task force, who had spent the better part of the night in bunkers and water-filled foxholes awaiting a follow-up VC infantry attack. At the same time, however, we were upset because they hadn't rousted us from sleep. No one had thought of us in their mad dash for foxholes and bunkers. So to the roll of thunder, the splashing of rain, the din of mortar shells, and the flash of explosions, we had slept through the first serious threat to the 1st Australian Task Force.

After the excitement of the 17th, 18 August began innocently enough for most of us. The men of B Company, who had been out since the morning of the 17th searching for the mortar and recoilless rifle firing positions and the VC who had shelled us, were returning to camp according to the battalion patrol plan. That afternoon D Company, replacing B Company, moved eastward from our base camp area into a rubber plantation a bit north of the abandoned village of Long Tan. As for me, I spent the day with Les Peters touring the C Company area and later walked over to the D Company area, which of course, because of the patrol, was almost devoid of personnel except for a few administrative people.

As D Company moved through the rubber plantation that rainy afternoon, it encountered a small group of VC, who rapidly fled. It moved out in pursuit, but the lead platoon soon came under intense fire from several sides and called in artillery fire. The other two platoons of D Company tried to aid the first but succeeded only in assisting in the withdrawal of the lead platoon survivors, then they too had to withdraw before the attacking enemy. As D Company reorganized, it found itself all but surrounded and greatly outnumbered. The New Zealand FO with the company continued to call in artillery fire (by now 161 Battery, the Australian artillery, and my own A Battery), bringing it in close around the defensive perimeter as the VC tried to overwhelm the men in assault after assault.

As the battle was just beginning, back at base camp most of the officers in the battalion HQ, including me, assembled at the officers' bar for a few beers. It was 3:30 or so in the afternoon.

54

We hadn't been there more than five or 10 minutes when a runner from the battalion TOC came charging over and told the 6RAR battalion commander, Lieutenant Colonel Townsend, that D Company had just made a really big contact in the rubber to the east of us. All of us to a man scrambled out of there and ran to our assigned areas for further orders. I tagged along to the TOC with the 6RAR commander and my boss, the 161 Battery commander. Inside the TOC everyone was working at fever pitch. They were in radio contact with D Company, the sounds of battle faintly audible as they transmitted to one another. As I remember, the D Company commander lost radio contact with his lead platoon, the one that first ran into the VC, and then lost contact with the platoon that had gone up to support the first. The radio blared with the pleading of operators attempting to raise the two platoons. Meanwhile, on the artillery radio net the D Company FO was calling in fire—first 161 Battery, then the Australian artillery, and then finally the big guns of my own battery. Even though the afternoon monsoon rains were coming down in sheets, we could hear the rumble and roar of Aussie and Kiwi 105s and of A Battery's six 155-mm howitzers as their shells screamed over our heads from the other side of the base camp to fall around the cut-off and surrounded D Company. The orders, appeals, and pleading over the radio continued as D Company tried to reestablish radio communications among themselves as well as calling for assistance from the battalion. The situation got so bad that at one point I heard a terror-stricken radio operator say, "They're gone!"

The 6RAR battalion commander reacted immediately. He ordered B Company to move to the battle area on foot through the jungle and A Company to assemble for movement by armored personnel carrier. The APCS soon arrived, and A Company with the 6RAR commander in charge roared off toward the battle. Meanwhile I stayed close to Major Honner, who was now on the artillery radio net directing artillery fire in conjunction with the D Company FO. They continued to ring D Company with hot steel. Furthermore, Major Honner began shifting the fires of A Battery in the hope of breaking up the enemy reserves. It was a tense time back at the artillery batteries as well. A Battery, for example, had expended most of the ammo near the guns, and all available men were now loading ammo from the dump on trucks, then literally kicking the hundred-pound shells back off the trucks near each of the firing howitzers.

Time passed and D Company began running out of ammo. Helicopters flew to the battle site with ammunition but had trouble delivering it because of the rain. Meanwhile the VC began to form for an assault on the rear of D Company. Over the radio came a call from the APCs bearing the battalion commander and A Company: "Inform American OP [observation post] officer [me] that his sergeant is with us." I couldn't believe it! In all the excitement my FO team reconnaissance sergeant had gotten his equipment together and gone with the APC and A Company reinforcements. I swore, assuring Major Honner that my sergeant was acting on his own and that when I got my hands on him, if he survived the battle, I'd court-martial him.

By now the APCs bearing A Company had reached the rubber plantation just south of where D Company lay, holding off repeated attacks. Into the rubber they roared, directly into several VC companies forming for assault. VC died all around as the machine guns of the APCs and the small arms of A Company did their job. Charlie broke and fled. The APCs, A Company, and finally B Company moving in from the base camp on foot all closed on the D Company perimeter. By this time it was probably about 6:00 or 7:00. The rest of the night they secured their positions and began removing the wounded Aussies by helicopter.

Back at base camp the artillery firing died down, and many of us retired to our tents to prepare for morning. At first light the rest of the battalion was to move into the battle area, discover whatever there was to discover, and hit the enemy again if possible. I must admit I was frightened over the whole prospect. We were not yet completely aware of what had happened, didn't know how many VC had been killed, and wondered whether the enemy was still there or had truly fled. In general, all we really knew was that most of D Company had been rescued, that the APCs with infantry and the artillery had saved the day, and that as soon as it was light we would have to go in and see the results of the battle for ourselves.

I spent the evening of 18 August preparing myself. I had never been out into the jungle before except for one little A Battery patrol, nor had I ever operated with the infantry. I had been with the infantry three whole days, and now it appeared my initiation would be an experience to equal the worst nightmares. I packed my gear, oiled my Owen submachine gun, removed each 9-mm round from the magazines, checked for cleanliness, and then reloaded. In my very careful preparations, however, I did forget something—my camera. To be honest, a camera was the furthest thing from my mind. I went to bed that night praying, finding some peace of mind in the biblical passage, "Take therefore no thought for the morrow: for the morrow shall take thought for the things of itself." Time and again during my year in Vietnam I found comfort in that simple verse, along with others from Matthew 6.

Early the next morning we boarded APCs and moved out through the jungle. As we approached the Suoi Da Bang River, just east of the base camp, the commander of the APC that my radio operator and I were riding on told us to take off our boots so we could swim better if our vehicle sank while fording. A lot of good that would have done me, since I couldn't swim at all. Regardless, I removed my boots and told Jim Gleason, my radio operator, to save my butt if we sank. There were no problems, however. We successfully forded the river and moved on toward the edge of the rubber plantation. There we were met by others—A Company, I think, because among them was my sergeant. He had survived the battle and was all smiles. I wanted to chew him out, but the sight of him, so pleased with himself, and the relief that thank God he was all right mellowed my anger. I don't remember saying a cross word to him then, nor did I ever mention the court-martial I had threatened the afternoon before.

Dismounting from the APCs, we moved into the rubber plantation, my FO section with the signal section of Major Honner. As we advanced through the rubber trees, American jet planes roared overhead, and for the first time I heard the sound of 20-mm Gatling guns being fired. The sound was like cloth tearing, not at all like rapid machine-gun firing. The Gatlings fired so fast that the sounds ran together. The aircraft were strafing possible enemy escape routes, I supposed. At the first sound of them we all hit the dirt and then, as we realized what it was, got up rather sheepishly and continued onward. Moving farther into the rubber, we made contact with D Company. Stories and rumors were rampant as old friends greeted one another and the D Company survivors related the events of the afternoon before.

As we established the battalion headquarters camp, the infantry companies and APCs roamed about us picking up VC bodies and burying them in shallow graves. They brought the VC weapons and other gear—SKS carbines, AK47 assault rifles, light machine guns, burp guns, American weapons, rocket-propelled grenade launchers, a mortar, recoilless rifles, a heavy machine gun on wheels, all kinds of ammunition and grenades, documents, a lot of web gear, and so on—to our site and deposited them in piles. It was interesting to watch the D Company personnel. They stood around the piles of booty in a proud, defiant way—as they well deserved to do, in my opinion. They had bravely met a horrible ordeal that had earned them the respect and admiration of us all.

One of our first tasks on reaching the battle site was to dig in, and dig in we did, worrying that perhaps the VC force would come back and take on the rest of us. For three days, 19, 20, and 21 August, we stayed at this location with the companies sweeping the area all around us for more VC, alive, wounded, or dead. The operation itself became known as "Operation Smithfield" in honor of the D Company commander, Major Smith. During these three days I did little except walk around a bit to look over the battle area and examine the booty. I even managed to write a letter home while sitting in the red mud of my foxhole.

Dear Frances,                                    Fri. 21 August 66
I haven't had a chance to write for a few days now, but things have been pretty hectic. By now you must have heard on the news of the big action we had here. The bn I'm with had a company get hit by a North Vietnamese [army] regular force of about two bns in strength [intelligence information later suggested a regiment of several NVA and VC main force battalions plus provincial VC D445 Battalion]. This resulted in some real hot action. This all happened about 48 hours ago. One of the Aussie platoons of 37 men was all but wiped out. We killed about 200 [245 actual], though in the process and there's probably another 400 wounded.

I'm writing from my foxhole out here in the middle of a rubber plantation. This is where the action took place. Yesterday and today we've spent picking up bodies and weapons and then burying the dead. Not a very nice job. Luckily I wasn't out with the company that got hit bad.

Early yesterday morning we swept through the area to see if we could find the cut-off members of an Aussie plt. and any more regulars. This is when we found the 200-odd North Vietnamese bodies, weapons, etc. Also, we found the cut-off Aussies. They were all lying facing where the enemy had been, bodies (VC) all around. Every single one of them was also dead, the officer that had been in charge also dead. They put up one heck of a fight. We also found several wounded regulars as we came through yesterday morning; three were taken alive.

Regardless of the poor conditions we've had here the last couple of days, believe it or not mail was delivered to us today. That sure makes it nice—keeps up morale.

Tomorrow we'll be going back into camp. We've done all we can, and Charlie's gotten away. Boy are we dirty. It's always muddy, and we're all mud from head to foot.

As I wrote the letter, incorrectly dated 21 August instead of 20 August, the view from my foxhole, or more accurately my slit trench, was anything but inspirational. The rubber trees all around me, shredded during the battle, still dripped white sap from their wounds. A few yards in front of me lay a bloated VC body with one arm pointing straight up toward the sky. To my rear lay piles of weapons, ammo, and equipment. And as always, members of D Company stood nearby guarding the entire area.

There was one pile of weapons that was especially depressing— the weapons of the D Company men who had been killed or wounded. Some were broken, stocks shattered by bullets or shrapnel and metal bent and twisted by the impact of lead and steel. In at least one case an SLR (the main rifle of the Aussie infantryman, 7.62-mm NATO) had its barrel bent. I don't know if it had been warped by heat, run over by an APC, or bent over the head of a threatening VC—I didn't ask. There were also a couple of M60 machine guns lying there. I was told that in some cases they had malfunctioned because the belts of ammo had gotten fouled by the mud during the battle.

During the first day at the battle site I saw one thing that smacked of Hollywood, though certainly what occurred was in dead earnest. An Aussie officer had begun interrogating the three enemy prisoners. He had two of them, one or both wounded as I remember, lying on the ground in front of him and was asking them all kinds of questions relating to intelligence. They refused to talk, so the Aussies took one off some distance and fired a pistol into the ground, simulating an execution. The plan, of course, was to make the other one think that if he didn't talk, he too would be shot. They asked more questions, and when the prisoner failed to respond, one Aussie resorted to standing on the guy's wounds. Though the VC was certainly in pain, I don't think he ever did give information of any consequence. Finally, interrogation complete, the Aussies removed the prisoners from the battle site.

The Aussies must have learned some valuable lessons from this battle, because in the days and weeks that followed certain changes began. For one thing, it became standard procedure for every machine gunner and machine-gun ammo bearer to encase the belt ammo he carried around his neck in rubber- or plastic-like tubes so it would stay clean even though the infantrymen might be lying in mud. Also, the 9-mm Owen submachine gun fell out of favor. Some Aussies carrying the Owen claimed that the little 9-mm slugs just didn't have the knockdown power required. In the coming weeks the Owen was gradually replaced by M16s that the Australian government began purchasing.

On 21 August Operation Smithfield ended. The area had been swept, bodies buried, and the captured weapons taken back to the task force area. Captured web gear, canteens, and other equipment were burned, and as we boarded the APCs to head back to the base camp, the pioneers (engineers) blew up a big pile of grenades. And what an explosion it was! The shrapnel flew dangerously close over our heads as we sat on top of our APCs. Everyone ducked, some swore, and I for one realized that there were a whole lot of ways to get killed in Vietnam, even by accident.

Dear Folks,                                          22 August 66

I just got back from the bush last night. We were in a rather nasty operation the last few days. I'm sure you've read about it in the papers, so I won't elaborate. Frances can tell you about some of the things. I came in with the infantry reinforcements about 10 hrs. later to mop up and so on. Boy, there sure were a lot of bodies. We counted 245 dead VC [and NVA] and captured three. It appears that we pretty well knocked the heck out of a bn and maybe more. We figure that the company (100 men) first hit must have been hit by a force of about 800–1,000 [closer to 1,500 it was estimated later]. We figure if the company hadn't run into them by luck that afternoon, they would have probably hit us here at camp (the task force). Of course they wouldn't have taken us, but we would have paid dearly, I'm afraid. Well, at any rate that should cut down any vc activity near here for a while.

Dear Frances,                                        22 August 66
    I'm afraid I may have told you a lot of nasty details about the whole thing in that letter I wrote from my foxhole. It wasn't too long after I finished that letter when we had another vc contact. Bn HQ was sitting there all alone (all the rifle companies were out) when suddenly one of our sentries saw six North Vietnamese moving toward us. He fired. They took off. Well, for about the next two hours we lay in our foxholes barely breathing, thinking that the whole big group of N. Viets would be down on us soon. It never happened. Now I really know what it's like to be scared. These infantrymen really have guts to go out day after day and night after night. I sure do admire them.

So ended my first experience with the infantry. Though I played no role in the battle itself, I was at least exposed in grand fashion to the horror of the real war. My FO team and I had seen a part of the war that no one else in A Battery would ever experience, nor in fact would anyone else in our entire battalion, 2/35th Artillery, during our year in Vietnam.
    As for the Australians, they killed more of the enemy in the battle of Long Tan than in the entire previous year or more. Though their losses were certainly a blow to the battalion at the time, the battle proved what they had known all along: that given the opportunity, the "digger" (Australian soldier) was a tremendous fighter. It was immediately obvious that the battalion took great pride in its accomplishment. Throughout my remaining time with 6RAR, the battle of Long Tan was an event the Aussies often referred to, and I think many hoped for another like it. As for me, what I saw at the battle site confirmed my worst fears of FOing with the infantry, and I spent the rest of my tour wondering when my turn would come to face the horror of such a battle.

# 5. **W**ITH **C** COMPANY 6RAR

On returning from Operation Smithfield, my job finally began to take form. I became a sort of artillery liaison officer to the Aussie 6RAR commander and to the New Zealand 161 Battery commander. Furthermore, I was to function as an FO for the infantry rifle companies whenever the need arose. The need arose almost immediately, and Major Honner, the 161 Battery commander, assigned me as FO to C Company 6RAR.

The 161 Battery FO with C Company, Captain Davis, was about to complete his 18-month tour of duty in Vietnam. All New Zealand tours of duty at this time were 18 months, and Major Honner, having no replacement for him, decided I should fill the gap. He ordered my FO section and me to move to C Company.

C Company became what I considered "my" infantry unit. Here they needed and used us in the capacity we had been trained for (more or less). After Captain Davis had gone, we were the FO team responsible for providing their artillery fire support. C Company was not entirely foreign to me. I had already met the company commander and the mortar FO, called Blue, and in the next days I met the rest of the company officers and top NCOs. The company second-in-command, or executive officer, was a quick-tempered but friendly person, probably in his early 30s. He and I got along exceptionally well, and during the next weeks we found time between patrols and operations to drink a lot of beer with the other company officers.

The three C Company platoon leaders were all young, the same age as me or younger, and all were second lieutenants. Second Lieutenant Eric Andrews, the most serious of the three, was a fantastic map reader, as I learned during Operation Vaucluse. Built like a weight lifter, he had gotten his education and the opportunity to become an army officer because of his football-playing ability (Australian rules football)—at least that's what I was told. Later in the year Eric became the battalion assistant adjutant, a job I think he welcomed in that it upped his chances for survival during the last months of his tour. A family man, he often talked about returning home, much as I did.

The other two platoon leaders were single, had no plans for marriage that I knew of, and never that I can remember showed any real desire for home. This was typical during my stay with the Aussies: I can't remember many of them expressing a longing to get home. A Battery personnel, on the other hand, were always talking about home. Perhaps, since I was sort of a foreigner, they just never saw fit to show me their real feelings. Or, maybe it was just their professionalism. Anyway, these two platoon officers were quite the guys—one tall, slim, dark, and rather serious looking, the other very young, short, muscular, and always smiling.

During my stay with C Company the officers were a tight and compatible little group. Months later, however, the lieutenants began dropping from the company. First one came down with malaria and had to be shipped back to Australia. While back home and on leave from the hospital, so I heard, he was hit and killed by a taxicab. Of the remaining two platoon leaders, the battalion assigned Eric to headquarters and the company commander relieved the other one of his duties. The last time I saw him, he was just hanging around battalion headquarters awaiting shipment home.

The C Company commander, a major, was an exceptional leader, and he commanded in a businesslike but personable way that made most subordinates want to please him and carry out his orders. He was probably in his mid- to late 30s, a bit paunchy, a chain-smoker who liked his rum and beer. But I never did meet an Aussie who didn't like to drink. During the weeks I worked for him, my respect and admiration for him as a leader grew tenfold. I was impressed by the way he could compel people to do their jobs without becoming angry, loud, or vulgar. Most Aussie officers seemed this way to me; always cool, deliberate, and extremely rational in their decision making, a far cry from the American leadership I had seen during my first year in the army.

The loud and blustery approach to leadership seemed to fall to the Aussie NCOs. Company Sergeant Major Harry Pope was top NCO in the company for a time and later, when headquarters posted him to the Australian Reinforcement Unit, we got a new CSM. The CSM of a company, much like the regimental sergeant major of the battalion, really ran the unit. The Aussie NCOs, like American NCOs, were the army's backbone and were the men who would respond to an officer's order or suggestion with "Right!" "All right mates, off your bloody arses and after the bastards!" One thing for certain, in a company or battalion the sergeant major was the next thing to God, and everyone had better believe it.

We had just joined C Company when the battalion alerted it for a three-day patrol. My FO team and I were to accompany the New Zealand FO (Captain Davis) and his team in supporting the C Company mission of searching out and making contact with the enemy regiment that had fled after the battle of Long Tan only a few days before. My God! I thought we had left that horrible experience behind us for good, and now here we were, going out to look for them again. On this patrol my team and I were merely to shadow the New Zealand section as a sort of on-the-job training. When we completed the patrol Captain Davis would depart, leaving me with sole FO responsibility for the company.

We prepared ourselves. We packed three days' rations (three Australian 24-hour packs), took four canteens each, ammunition, extra socks, water purification tablets, cigarettes, and other equipment. As time went on during my stay with the infantry, I learned what to take, how to pack it, and how to carry all that gear in the most comfortable way. Wearing gear was an individual matter, and each person rapidly discovered for himself what was workable and comfortable.

The C Company commander briefed us and designated our route of march. Our initial route was to be basically the same one D Company had taken a few days before, back through that dreaded rubber plantation battleground. The briefing was thorough, the plan was well thought out, and at its conclusion we officers dropped the formalities and broke out the beer.

We left base camp on the morning of 24 August, passed through the perimeter wire, and headed out of our rubber plantation home into a grove of banana trees. Whether the bananas were wild or had been planted by the local Vietnamese I don't know, but on our way out we sampled some and found them extremely sweet. I was surprised at their size—they weren't more than four inches long.

We continued east, away from base camp, to the Suoi Da Bang River. A few days before we had forded this river with APCs on our way to the Long Tan battle area, but this time we crossed over on a log. I was apprehensive to say the least, considering that the river was deep in spots and I couldn't swim—not that you could have anyway, carrying ammunition, three days' rations, and other equipment. But I made it across.

From the river we moved through scrub jungle and tall grass into the rubber plantation itself and the battle area. Everyone was tense; I think we all expected that NVA–VC main force–D445 regiment to be there again. As we moved through, battle signs were still obvious. Slit trenches and machine-gun positions that the VC had dug near a small hut were still there, expended rifle and machine-gun shell casings lay all around, and the trees still bled white rubber sap from the wounds inflicted by artillery shell bursts, grenade fragments, and small arms fire. It was so quiet. My God, I was scared! I'm sure all of us were even more afraid than we had been a few days before. Then we had been a whole battalion; now we were only one small infantry company.

As we moved on through the rubber, the smell of death was still there. I was to observe several times in the coming weeks and months that death produced a strange, sweet, sickening smell, the smell of blood and flesh in a hot climate, I suppose. Finally we got through most of the rubber and stopped briefly on the edge for a smoke. Here the trees were completely chewed up by artillery fire. Someone told me this was where fire from my battery had hit the VC reserves that were forming for another attack. I had not seen this part of the battlefield during Operation Smithfield.

From this point on we tried to follow blood trails. Some of the trails were heavy, although the monsoon rains had washed most away. On at least one occasion the lead platoon probed in freshly dug dirt and I think found a couple of bodies that had been hurriedly buried during the retreat. Once, in an area where artillery had fired on a suspect VC escape route, we found a dead bush deer. I was amazed at how small it was, like a medium-sized dog.

As evening approached we "hoochied up" (made camp) and established our perimeter defense. I found this phase quite an ordeal. In whatever light remained, we had to eat, dig in, plan defensive artillery fires, send the preplanned concentrations back to the Australian Artillery Regiment headquarters (1st Field Regiment, Royal Australian Artillery) in code over the radio, and put up a shelter complete with mosquito net. In this area we absolutely had to use our nets; the mosquitoes here carried an especially bad strain of malaria. I was told that just a few weeks before a patrol out in this area hadn't used their nets and were bitten up by mosquitoes. Some of the men got malaria, and one had died.

During this evening make-camp period, I soon learned the advantage Aussie and New Zealand officers had in having batmen. Because their batmen dug them in, put up their shelters, and cooked their food, they could concentrate on the important tasks of establishing the perimeter and so on. As for me, I had to do everything myself. As time went on, however, my radio operator and I learned to cooperate in these things, giving me a little more time for artillery fire planning, the nightly briefing by the company commander, and such.

Getting settled for the night was an art to be learned. The two lightweight shelter halves we each carried were easily snapped together and strung up with pieces of nylon cord tied to trees, bushes, or whatever was at hand. In the jungle there was no problem finding something to tie the cords on. When time permitted and it wasn't too wet, many men dug shallow sleeping holes (graves, some called them) under this shelter. The thinking was that if we were attacked at night, a sleeping hole would serve as a fighting hole as well as protection against the initial attack. Down in the sleeping holes we placed our air mattresses, and over them, we hung our mosquito nets, tied to convenient little loops inside the shelter halves.

The rations we carried were not American C rations but Aussie 24-hour packs. Each pack of three meals took up little more room in our backpacks than one meal of American Cs. The packs held three tuna-fish-sized cans of bully beef or mutton, little sausages, and bacon with eggs. The rest of the ration pack contained bags of tea and sugar, a dried fruit bar, and a tube of sweet cream. Though these packs were certainly not as high-quality as American Cs, at least in my opinion, we could carry more of them and thus could operate out in the jungle for days at a time without resupply by helicopter, a tactic the Aussie infantry used consistently and, I believe, successfully. We heated our rations and brewed our tea on a little tin fold-up stove that each of us carried or on a stove made from an empty ration can, using the heat tablets we carried. Those little square white tablets were great. We just broke off a piece, placed it on the ground, in the stove, or in the makeshift can stove, lit it, and put food and brew (tea or coffee) on to heat. Seldom did we eat cold rations or not take time for a hot cup of tea while in the jungle.

After it was dark that first night, the company commander asked me to fire in some artillery concentrations from A Battery. He wanted me to bring the fire in especially close to our perimeter, explaining that the company was fearful of artillery landing too close. I think this was his way of letting the troops know I was OK, that I knew what I was doing, and that artillery fire even from the big American 155s could be trusted.

I had never before brought in fire in these circumstances, where I couldn't adjust by sight but would have to rely on map and sound. The jungle here was so thick you couldn't see more than 10 or 15 feet up or in any direction around. I called over the radio for the first rounds, a battery one round (one shell fired simultaneously by each of the six howitzers), on a spot I thought was about 1,500 meters from our location. The first rounds were a lot closer than I expected—at least they sounded close, probably only 1,000 meters away. From there I walked them in toward us until I could see the explosions flash through the jungle and hear shrapnel hitting the trees overhead. Some of the people on the outer edge of our perimeter began complaining, but the company commander told them on the radio to hug the dirt and ordered me to bring the fire in closer. I suppose I finally walked the fire to within 150 meters before we decided it was close enough. The troops were impressed that such big artillery could be brought in so close with such accuracy. My position as C Company FO was confirmed and accepted, I think, that first night.

The second day out, at one point we had to cross a clearing to get to another patch of jungle on the other side. The lead platoon had already crossed, and the next platoon and company HQ (my location) remained just on the other side of the clearing. The third platoon brought up our rear. The company commander told our New Zealand FO to put some artillery fire out front of the lead platoon on the other side of the clearing and off into the jungle as a precautionary measure. Captain Davis called in fire from the New Zealand 161 Battery. As the first rounds started to come in, something sounded wrong; they seemed much too close. Sure enough, some of the rounds landed not ahead of the lead platoon, on the other side of the clearing and off into the jungle, but in the clearing itself between them and us. Captain Davis shouted into the radio trying to get them to stop shooting. Apparently a couple of the six guns firing were off. Of course when one is firing at a distance of six or seven miles, a little error on the artillery piece itself is a big error out in the target area. The fire finally stopped, and we moved on through the clearing in single file without further incident. An accident similar to this months later had a more unfortunate ending for D Company 6RAR. A mistake on the guns made the shells drop right into company headquarters, killing and wounding several. An acquaintance of mine, the D Company 2IC, was among the wounded and lost a leg.

As a whole, the patrol turned out to be uneventful, and we could not find the remnants of the NVA-VC regiment—thank goodness! Finally, on the third day, we circled around and once again swept back through the rubber plantation of the Long Tan battlefield. This time our move through was horrible: the smell was indescribable. Wild hogs had dug up some of the VC bodies and fed on them, and hot weather had done the rest.

Apart from that the trip was easy. We moved west through the scrub and grass, recrossed the river, went through the banana trees, and came back into the friendly shelter of our rubber plantation base camp home. As we passed through the perimeter wire we unloaded our weapons, then broke file and headed for the comfort of our tents, a cold beer, and a shower by canvas bucket. We were dirty and tired, but at least still all in one piece. As for me, I now felt more like a veteran. Besides, I was a year older, almost! The next day, the 27th, was my 24th birthday.

Unhappily I discovered that afternoon what happens to feet if wet boots and socks are not removed for several days. I had been so fearful of night attack during this patrol that I hadn't taken my boots off at all, and now after three days and nights of muddy, wet feet, I had a problem. The boots came off all right, but as I pulled off my socks, part of my feet came with them. The skin just peeled off. My feet were brown and wrinkled, and my toe-

1. Dear Frances: The photo of my wife I carried during my Vietnam tour of duty (studio unknown)

2. Dear Folks: My parents, Elva and Leo Steinbrook, Christmas 1966

3. The Nui Dinh hills, 9,000 meters west of the 1ATF base camp at Nui Dat

4. One of A Battery's six 155-mm self-propelled howitzers ready for a fire mission

5A. A Battery FOS: Lieutenant Roy Minick

5B. A Battery FOS: me

Vung Tau and the South China Sea ahead
om the air

7. A Battery FO team with C Company 6RAR
(*from left*): PFC Jim Gleason, Sergeant Frank
Beltier, and me

C Company 6RAR infantrymen returning to
se camp after a three-day patrol

9. Somewhere in the Nui Dinh hills during
Operation Vaucluse, I radio 161 Battery Royal
New Zealand Artillery

10. Australian 105-mm howitzer and crew ready for action (*photograph by Chuck Heindrichs*)

11. Freshly showered after a five-day patrol with A Company 6RAR, I pose outside my base camp tent

12. A Battery lieutenants (*from left*) Chuck Heindrichs, me, Harry Litchfield (*kneeling*), Roy Minick, and Doug Mistler

13. Australian 1st APC Squadron vehicles fitted with twin .30-caliber machine-gun turrets

14. Australian 81-mm mortar, APC, and crew shortly before hitting a road mine during Operation Ingham, wounding four

15. Large VC rice and supply cache discovered during Operation Ingham

16. Early morning, the day before Christmas 1966, I return from a successful night ambush

17. Element of A Battery's 11th Armored Cavalry convoy escort coming home from Operation Junction City

18. Operation Portsea at a fire support base
(*from left*): Lieutenant Harry Litchfield, an
Aussie mate, and me

19. A Battery's M557 tracked command post
carrier Fire Direction Center vehicle dug in and
sandbagged at an Operation Portsea fire support
base

nails were green. After a while they dried, but then they began to peel some more. No permanent problem resulted, however, and I learned yet another lesson the hard way.

Dear Folks,                                             28 August 66

Another month is drawing to a close. Yesterday some of the Aussie officers and sgts. threw me a little birthday party. I got two presents, a bag of candy and a chocolate bar. At least it gave everyone something to do for a while. This was all at C Company 6RAR. I'm living with the infantry now, you know, and going out mainly with C Company on operations. I just got back from a three-day patrol with them a day or two ago. That jungle is really something, kind of beautiful in a way. I believe I lost about five to 10 lbs. in that three days.

Tomorrow my FO section and myself are going to Vung Tau for three days of rest and recuperation. We'll stay in a big U.S. R&R center and just purely relax for three days. If a person didn't do this once in a while, everyone would go mad. I don't know which is worse, being in a jungle or being back here bored to death.

Dearest Frances,                                        30 August 66

Yesterday, today, and tomorrow are days of rest for me and my section. We were given a three-day pass in Vung Tau. I'm staying in a villa used for a BOQ by [U.S.] officers stationed in Vung Tau. These officers really have it made. Their rooms are as nice as any Holiday Inn room, with maid service, etc. All they do is go to work every day—just like a civilian job. They go to a big officers' club every night, see movies, lie on the beach, and are in zero danger of ever getting shot at so long as they don't fool around downtown. This is what I could have had in Vietnam had I been in an administrative branch of the army. What's really sickening is that one of the captains here got married to his girl a week ago. She's an army nurse and got stationed here with him. So now since they're together here they got married and are having a real good time. To them it's just a year-long honeymoon in a tropical paradise. What did I do to deserve combat rather than this, honey? Of course time goes slower for these people, but what the heck, it's a clean and safe year for them.

About R&R, I think you'd better check into both Japan and Hawaii just to be safe, especially if you need a passport. It takes a while to get one, you know, so if needed for one or the other you'd better get it.

30 August 66

This is my second letter to you today. What's the first anniversary gift supposed to be, paper? I can't remember, but I got you a little something anyway [a Vietnamese doll]. Hope you like it.

When I was buying the gift, a boy approached me and asked if I wanted to buy some "f--k pictures." Well, you know curious me, I just had to see what the heck he was selling. Good Lord, were they detailed. Really, it's too bad, I'd bet money like that wasn't made before Americans came here. We may be doing the Vietnamese people some good, but I guess we're corrupting them at the same time.

The Australians were good about rotating their men into Vung Tau every once in a while. I didn't realize it at first, but the battalion operated on a planned program of patrolling. Each company had responsibility during a certain time for patrolling between operations, and when any free time presented itself, as many men as possible were sent to the beaches of Vung Tau for a few days. Since Vung Tau was only 25 miles to the south, it was simply a matter of catching a supply convoy or maybe even a helicopter for the ride in.

Vung Tau was a shock. I'd been there during our staging at Bien Hoa, when we had been trying to make logistics arrangements, but I had never really seen any part of it except the ammo dump, airfield, and other supply points. Even while flying out of Vung Tau with 161 Recce Flight, I had been exposed only to the airfield area and their base camp down on the beach. But now I saw the whole thing. Vung Tau was like another world. Once there, it was hard to imagine that just a few miles away and only days before we had been walking through the jungle, cleaning up after a battle, and retching at the smell of decomposing flesh. Here in Vung Tau soldiers wore clean, starched fatigues, lived in billets equivalent to Stateside barracks, lay on the beaches, went to the post exchange, and for the most part didn't even carry weapons. Some officers lived in beautiful old French villas, had maids, ate the best food, and spent most evenings at the Vung Tau officers' club.

The PX area along the airfield was one of the biggest shocks. It had a snack bar where you could buy hot dogs, hamburgers, cheeseburgers, malts, and shakes. It seemed unfair that some spent the war in this atmosphere and others of us were doomed to the mud, jungles, and horror of the real war.

My visits downtown were as memorable as my French villa BOQ was comfortable. The marketplace especially was a place of wonder, excitement, filth, and smell, and an education in free trade. They sold everything—fresh meat (though not by my standards), fruits, vegetables, tobacco, cooked food, and of course thousands and thousands of items made especially for visiting GIs. Furthermore, you couldn't walk a block without being approached by a little boy or girl asking, "Hey, GI, you want number one girl?" And if a GI said no, as I think few did, the little guy or gal would say, "You cheap Charlie, number 10 GI, number 10,000 GI." As for me, I can't say I was even tempted to indulge myself. It was simply a matter of personal self-discipline and morality.

The big officers' club in Vung Tau was nice even by Stateside standards. There you could dine much as you might back home, get a mixed drink at the bar, and play the slot machines. Slot machines? There they were, five- and 10-cent slot machines. I must have spent one whole afternoon at them, losing 30 dollars or so. The whole place reminded me of Miami Beach. It was right down on the shore, only a few yards from the South China Sea. And just around the corner were the bars, the shops, and the massage parlors. That section of Vung Tau teemed with GIs, plus a few Koreans, Australians, and New Zealanders. There was no question but that these enterprises were making money hand over fist. Hawkers stood in the doorways trying to entice soldiers, some on pass like me, and others the starched-uniform garrison troopers of Vung Tau. They didn't have any problem. Bars were full, the music was loud, and the massage parlors worked overtime. The price was right! Booze was high, but a massage with all the trimmings was relatively cheap, depending on the client's desires. Many of my Aussie mates went to great lengths describing the options available for the different prices.

For me at least, the greatest pleasure of the three days in Vung Tau was my big double bed in the villa. There I slept late on clean white sheets in a room with electric lights, a bath, windows, and a clean tile floor. I could just lie there and stare up at the ceiling without having to peer through mosquito netting. Nor, when I finally got around to getting dressed, did I have to first empty my boots and check for crawling wildlife. It was simple things like these that made the three days a paradise, a respite from the pressures of the jungle at Nui Dat.

The time finally came, however, to put fatigues and gear back on and convoy "home." Flak vests and helmets in place, weapons loaded and ready, we began the return journey. Away from the villa we rode, past the airfield and nearby PX, past the naval storage yards, and out onto a highway clogged with military vehicles, French cars, and little Vietnamese Lambretta buses always loaded to the maximum with people or market goods. Up the road north, first through the suburbs of Vung Tau, and then onto open road flanked first by swamp and later by the endless green rice paddies. Onward north through the villages along Highway 15, a turn at Phuoc Le, up Highway 52 a bit farther, and finally onto Highway 2 and the last miles to Nui Dat, the dimness beneath the rubber trees, and the sandbagged and dirt-packed floor of my C Company tent.

Dearest Frances,                                    4 September 66

In a few days we're going out into the bush again. I probably won't get back until near the end of Sept. I'm afraid my letters will be darn few and far between until then. I imagine that we'll be pretty busy; however, I will write as much as I can. One good thing, the month will go fast. Then we'll have only 2¾ months to wait until we can be together on R&R.

6 September 66

Another very boring day here in camp. When we're not out in the bush we do absolutely nothing; we just sit around and read, smoke, and drink coffee [not to mention shifts in the company command post and planning artillery fire for ongoing patrolling and ambushes].

This month will go fast. We'll be out beating the bush for at least two weeks solid without ever coming in for clean clothes or showers or anything. Needless to say, I'm not looking forward to that at all, but time will fly. Because of this I'm afraid you won't get many letters. I'll be lucky to get a couple written the whole time. I may write later this evening, and for sure tomorrow.

I never did get around to writing later on the 6th, or the next day, or for that matter until 29 September. Things simply got too busy. Operation Vaucluse into the Nui Dinh (Baria) hills was about to get under way, and I had briefings to attend, maps to study, and gear to pack.

# 6. OPERATION VAUCLUSE AND FINAL DUTIES WITH C COMPANY

Dearest Frances,                               29 September 66

I really hated not being able to write you the last three weeks. We just got in from the operation [Operation Vaucluse], you know. It sure is good to be back. The first thing we all did was to take a shower. We hadn't had one bath or any clean clothes the whole time. Boy, were we grubby.

The whole operation started off the 8th of Sept. The whole battalion was loaded on helicopters that day, and we were dropped off into the middle of the jungle about 10 miles north of here. From there we moved to the base of the Baria [Nui Dinh] hills (mountains). The whole of the operation from then on consisted of assaulting up and down mountains, ridge lines, and valleys. Talk about being pooped, well I've never climbed mountains before and hope I don't have to too much more, especially this kind. Not only are they steep and you begin to feel like a mountain goat, but also every inch of them is covered with heavy jungle, bamboo, vines, etc. There were times when we were so darn cold and wet and dirty that we all couldn't have cared less if Charlie had hit us, and hit us he did. Our third day out Charlie hit us five times. The first time we were just walking along and all of a sudden four vc hit our forward platoon. Nobody was hurt, and we got no vc. Then we moved on top of a small ridge and set up camp, intending to spend the night there. This was about noon. The medic and I were sort of laughing and talking about how there probably weren't any Charlie in our area; well, just about then four more vc walked up to a machine gunner about 30 yds. away from us, and all hell broke loose again. Once again, no casualties on either side. After things were calm we ate lunch and I went back up to the medic, and we were joking about how we *thought* there were no vc around earlier and how we had gotten hit just then. Well once again, as we shot the bull, Charlie hit us, this time pretty hard. Boy, did I do the fast 40-yard crawl back to my radio and weapon. I've never tried to get so low to the ground in all my life, because the old bullets were really whipping overhead. You should have seen my [New Zealand] radio operator shake from fright, but all the time just talking on the radio as calm as could be. This time we lost one of our people, but still got no vc. Our man that was hit was pretty bad off, but he'll be all right. Well, we had a couple more contacts at that same spot that day, but from then on out we had none until about two days before we came back here. It's funny, though, but all those times we were hit not once did I actually see Charlie; in fact, only one or two people did. All you see is movement in the bushes or something like that. The heck of it is they're shooting at you from about 20 yds. away. I guess that's the war here, unless of course they hit you in large numbers.

So far as we know now, there will be no big operation until about the end of Oct. again. Of course we'll be going out on ambush patrols every so often, I suppose, but that's not too bad. Believe it or not, honey, I sort of like the job now. In this type of job you really know you're fighting a war. If I were back at the btry, I would never know the real war that the infantry fights, the type that a person reads about and sees movies about. I'm glad that I'm having this experience; however, now that I've seen it, I would like to get back to the btry. In Dec. I'll be back and no more foing for me except maybe from the air once in a while.

Yesterday I found out that I'm probably the first and only American ever to be attached to a New Zealand arty btry and then reattached to an Aussie infantry company. As far as they know, this never ever happened even during wwii or the Korean War. I feel kind of proud. Under their system a capt. is supposed to do this job of foing, so actually I'm filling a capt. slot. All the other fos with the infantry here [6rar and 5rar] are New Zealand and Australian captains [and some senior first lieutenants]. Well, at least in another month I'll be a 1st lt.

I think we can plan on being in Hawaii for Christmas; however, just to be safe, please get your visa and passport for Japan. It sure can't hurt to be extremely safe.


Operation Vaucluse had involved more than I told Frances in my letter. It was a rather lengthy excursion into a range of small mountains that the vc had held for years. As far as I know, no Australian had been in the area before, unless it had been the Special Air Service on one of their long-range reconnaissance patrols. Our mission was to find out what was in those hills and to disrupt the vc observation that we suspected was being conducted from those heights, the most prominent in the entire province.

Preparations for the operation began weeks before 8 September. Intelligence information had to be collected, the scheme of battalion maneuvers worked out, and support requirements laid on. Then, after all the preliminary work was done, battalion headquarters assigned company missions and held briefings.

One of the preoperation briefings centered on a topographical sandbox model of the Nui Dinh hills created by members of the 6RAR intelligence section. It was beautiful. They had even stretched wires over the box to form the military map 1,000-meter grid squares corresponding to those on our 1:50,000 and 1:25,000 scale military maps. It was a work of art that took them days and days. It gave all of us a feel for the area before we ever set foot in it. Important as the sandbox was, however, it became the butt of many a joke. The sight of intelligence section personnel "playing" in the sandbox drew smiles from most of us. But it was all in fun. We knew how hard they had worked and how important it was to us all.

My FO team for this operation was larger than normal. Since my reconnaissance sergeant had been taken ill, leaving only Jim Gleason, my radio operator, and myself on the team, we were augmented by Blue, the Aussie mortar platoon FO ; Woodie, a New Zealand radio operator from Captain Davis's old FO section; Coy, our company Vietnamese interpreter; and one C Company medic. It was a great crew, as I discovered during the operation, and I became especially fond of Woodie, my teenage New Zealand radio man.

Each of us carried seven days' rations at the beginning of this operation. The battalion wanted to maneuver for as long as possible without the giveaway of helicopter resupply. I had turned in my Owen submachine gun for this operation, deciding that this small weapon was not right for me. Instead I carried my M14, the standard U.S. Army NATO 7.62-mm rifle. This was my A Battery issue weapon, I was adept at using it, and I knew it had all the power I would need in any situation. It wasn't until November that I temporarily got an M16. American artillery outfits were low on the M16 priority list; the infantry was fully equipped with them first. The Aussies themselves were only beginning to acquire them. In fact, A Battery still hadn't gotten the M16 by the time I left Vietnam in May 1967.

Operation Vaucluse began with all of 6RAR marshaling down in a flat area northwest of the battalion base camp and just south of 5RAR. Eventually, about March or April 1967, this site became Luscombe Field, the task force airstrip and new home of 161 Recce Flight with their Cessna fixed-wing aircraft and the little bubble-front (Sioux) helicopters, or Possums as they were fondly called. Here, in the morning hours of 8 September, flight upon flight of Hueys came down to receive each of our rifle companies and the battalion headquarters. After a short wait my section, the C Company commander, his radio operators, and I climbed aboard our chopper. Doors open and loaded to capacity, we sat or sprawled wherever there was room. There were no seats or seat belts. I remember hoping the pilot wouldn't execute a sharp right or left bank and lose us before we ever reached the landing zone. It was an awesome sight, all those Hueys carrying us, a company at a time, into hostile territory like a huge swarm of olive-colored dragonflies. And the noise! No one who was in Vietnam will ever forget the sound of the Huey.

In a very short time our company approached the LZ. In unison our choppers briefly touched down, and we hurriedly jumped out into the tall grass. There was no opposition to our landing as the entire battalion disembarked and began moving off into the surrounding shrub jungle company by company. The area was very soggy, with a heavy layer of dead vegetation covering the ground. The jungle itself was fairly thick but not as tall as most. We moved out, company on line, platoons one behind the other, and each of us moving quietly along in single file, a configuration that was almost essential to maintain control and avoid becoming separated and lost.

We hadn't gone far when I began to get an uncomfortable tickling sensation on the inside of my legs and around my crotch. Apparently others were having the same experience, because it wasn't long before we were ordered to halt. While some remained on the alert, the rest of us removed our gear and dropped our pants to see what was causing the tickling. Horror of horrors! My legs and crotch, and everyone else's, were covered with little leeches. We promptly began to burn them off one another with cigarettes, pull them off, or squirt them with insect repellent. We must have been the most laughable sight in Vietnam. There we were, over 100 combat soldiers, armed to the teeth, at least half of us with our pants down, bare-butted and picking little leeches off our legs and private parts. Though it seems funny now, at the time I didn't see anyone laughing. After ridding ourselves of the little devils and soaking our boot tops and pants legs with insect repellent, we moved on. This one leech stop did not end our problem, however; before we made it out of that soggy area we stopped several more times. Despite tucked-in pants legs well saturated with repellent, those little leeches somehow persisted in getting in and heading for the warmth of the crotch.

Our landing zone had been about 5,000 to 6,000 meters northeast of the base of our objective, the Nui Dinh hills. We spent two days moving very slowly toward them, through swampy ground, leeches, scrub jungle, and small paddies. Little did I comprehend then that this was the easy part. Early on the first day, we found we had to cross a stream. We usually just waded across and hoped there were no deep places. In this case, however, the stream lay at the bottom of a ravine, maybe 15 or 20 feet down. There was no way of sliding down one bank and climbing the other, so the Aussies felled a tree across the top with the idea that we would walk across it. Right! Just what I had always wanted to do, walk a log 15 feet over a swift-running river in enemy territory, carrying 30 pounds or so of equipment, and me a nonswimmer at that. What the hell! My attitude in the past weeks had become such that at this point one little log over a river couldn't terrify me. Once again I warned the people around me that I couldn't swim, and then I headed across the wet log. No problem! Some of the guys did fall in, however. And this was not the last river we crossed. In the weeks ahead we waded others, the water often higher than our belt buckles. All the while, I wondered why I had never learned to swim.

As we moved along that first day. A Company ran into several Viet Cong. The firefight was brief, and neither they nor the vc suffered any casualties. We also had a brief, inconsequential fight. As evening approached, we drew up in a jungle area about 2,000 to 3,000 meters from the base of the hills and established camp. As usual we put up shelter halves, heated food, brewed tea, and planned our defenses. The ground was so soggy that on this night I didn't bother digging a sleeping hole for fear water would seep in. As it turned out, I might just as well have dug one; I wouldn't have gotten any wetter. Apparently I had put my hooch in a slight ground depression, because during the middle of the night, as the monsoon rains began to fall, I found myself trying to sleep in a pool of water that ran up over my air mattress. What a night! I tossed, turned, and dreamed while the water ran under and around my body. I believe it was the most miserable night I've ever spent. Then toward morning, uncomfortable as I already was, the ground began to tremble. As the ground shook, literally bouncing me around in my pool of water, I realized what was going on. B-52s were bombing the Nui Dinh hills in preparation for our move into them. They must have been dropping thousand-pounders the way it felt. Later on, when I saw the craters, I wondered if the bombs had been even larger.

Our second day out was uneventful except that one man stumbled into a nest of jungle bees. The poor guy had to be medevaced (evacuated) because the bees had stung him on the throat and breathing became almost impossible. That night we hoochied up right at the base of the hills. Not wanting to locate myself in a depression again I, with several others, chose to roost on a little rocky knoll. This didn't work either. About the middle of the night I awakened in a slanted position to discover that one of my three air mattress inserts had deflated, probably punctured by a sharp rock. I lay there the rest of the night on a bed about 18 inches wide, not daring to roll over for fear I'd roll right out of my hooch and down the knoll into who knows what.

On 10 September we were pushed to our physical limits. That was the day we struggled almost 2,000 feet up a mountain through bamboo, vines, and jungle such as I had never seen. The climb in the heat with all that equipment was almost more than a body could endure. I hadn't worked that hard since high-school football practice. Charlie didn't help matters either. First A Company encountered and killed one VC, then we ran into them off and on a couple of times. Once, as the firing grew at our point, I would have been quite content to hug the dirt and simply ready my artillery in case it was needed. But instead, the company commander ordered us to advance, so advance into the firefight we did, at a half crouch. Shortly, Charlie broke off the engagement, leaving no casualties. We suffered none either. Another series of firefights occurred later in the afternoon on the ridgeline, the contacts I reported in my letter to Frances, but there too we failed to score a kill. Unfortunately we lost one man, and I learned the hard way always to stay near my radio and to carry my weapon at all times.

My New Zealand radio operator, Woodie, functioned coolly during these brief firefights. At one point during the longest fight, I ordered him to raise the battery on the radio. Though his hands were shaking violently and he could hardly hold the radio handset to his mouth, he spoke as calmly as if he were back in base camp talking about his "bird" (girl) in Vung Tau. He was an experienced and brave little guy; this was old hat to him by now. He'd been in Vietnam better than a year, had been with Captain Davis for a long time, and had been in many a firefight some months back when 1RAR, the first Aussie infantry battalion in Vietnam, supported by 161 Battery, had conducted joint operations with the 173d Airborne Brigade in the Iron Triangle north of Saigon.

In the succeeding days we walked, patrolled, walked, and then walked some more, always fighting the jungle with its creepers and vines. There were more contacts with Charlie, but A Company got all the kills, as I remember. And we discovered and destroyed VC camps and supplies.

As we moved through the hills, I was surprised at the size of the B-52 bomb craters—15 feet or so deep and what looked like 20 yards across. At the site of one crater we found bits and pieces of clothing, some a little sticky, and one complete shirt pocket with a comb still buttoned inside. The interesting thing was that a South Vietnamese shoulder patch was still attached to one bit of clothing. What would a South Vietnamese soldier be doing up there among the Viet Cong? Well, perhaps a shirt had been stolen, or maybe one had come up here for R&R, or maybe he was just visiting relatives! We made all kinds of jokes, for few of us had any real confidence in the loyalty of South Vietnamese soldiers.

During our second week in the hills, I came close to getting shot because of my own stupidity. We had finally been resupplied and, in the best British military tradition, had gotten our rum ration. The CSM distributed the rum by pouring a small amount into each man's canteen cup as he came by. The company commander got a whole bottle for officers' consumption. As usual, after we had dug in and hoochied up for the night, we officers met with the major to plan and discuss the night's defenses, artillery concentrations, and our activities for the next day. As we planned, we nipped on the officers' rum. Planning finished, I got up to head over to my hooch, but the commander stopped me. At the time I thought there was some additional planning to do. Instead, he broke out the rum bottle again and suggested we sit awhile longer and talk. Talk and drink we did, and I became a little light-headed. It had gotten dark by the time we finished socializing, and as I attempted to return to my hooch I realized it would be pure luck if I ever found it. It was so dark I couldn't see a thing, not even my hands as I put them out in front of me to keep from walking into trees. Had I known earlier I'd be moving after dark, I would have shot a direction between my area and the company command post with my compass and counted the number of paces between. But I hadn't, so it was up to instinct to lead me back. I headed off through the pitch-black jungle in what I thought was the correct direction. I did go the right way, but in the darkness I overshot my hooch and wandered out onto the perimeter. "Ow!" I stepped on someone. Click! Just as I stepped on him, I heard him click off the safety of his rifle. I remember thinking I was dead and then instinctively and almost instantly saying in a loud whisper, "It's Yank!" The C Company digger didn't shoot. Since everyone knew me as "Yank" and since my presence was unusual, I had chosen the right response in this ridiculous situation and probably saved my skin. He asked what my problem was; I told him, and he led me right to my hooch. I thanked him and later, in the total darkness of the jungle, safely tucked in under my mosquito net, I said a little prayer of thanks and vowed that I'd never again pull such an idiotic stunt.

In our wanderings through the hills during the almost three weeks of the operation, there were many other incidents that, though not important, I will always remember. For example, one day while we were moving down a footpath through heavy jungle, a small creature darted in front of me. It was a deer no larger than a very small dog. I'd seen pictures of miniature jungle deer years before, but seeing one alive gave me a thrill. Another time, at night, a sentry saw what he thought was a vc coming down the trail. He shot, saw it go down, then waited until morning to confirm his kill. Morning came, and there in the path lay a large apelike creature—an orangutan, some said. I didn't see it myself.

Then, too, there was the problem of smoking at night. Some of us, while in Vietnam, developed a tremendous cigarette habit. For us night, and the standing order that no one was to smoke, was difficult. My solution—dig a smoking hole. On one occasion I dug a hole five feet deep, crawled inside, put one shelter half over the top, and started to smoke. The trouble was lack of air. When I finally came up to breathe by raising the top covering, I probably sent up smoke signals.

The Australians were unique in some of their ways, even out in the jungle. The tradition of rum ration, for example, was clung to. And the gentleman-officer image was maintained. Each morning every officer shaved. It meant heating water before chow and sacrificing an early brew, but we all did it. It was just another way of saying, "Things are normal, no problem, carry on lads!" Our tea breaks were yet another part of this overall calmness, orderliness, and refusal to show fear or concern. If the opportunity presented itself and there was no particular hurry, we'd stop, light a heat tablet, and in no time have a steaming canteen cup of hot, dark tea laced with sugar and sweet cream. I never ceased to admire how nonchalantly the Aussies and Kiwis approached every task or problem. I often wondered whether it was in their nature or was the result of hundreds of years of military and colonial tradition taught as the acceptable way of approaching any situation. Frankly, it seemed the intelligent approach to leading combat troops.

My opinion of American C rations and my taste for them changed considerably during the operation. Before joining the Aussie infantry, I had always regarded C rations as one of the hardships that had to be endured in the army. Though I didn't dislike them, I can't say I enjoyed them either. My infantry experience with the Aussies changed all that. After a steady diet of Australian 24-hour packs with their bully beef and mutton, sausages, and dried fruit bars, American C rations were a gourmet's delight. When resupplied with Cs and 24-hour packs on, I think, the eighth day, we devoured the Cs immediately. Even the Aussies found Cs superior, but with the requirement of carrying so many days' rations, the bulky C rations just weren't acceptable. If we did carry them, we took only the main part and discarded the extras.

Our water supply in the jungle was generally good. There seemed always to be a stream where we could fill our canteens, or water bottles, as the Aussies called them. The water for the most part was clean and cool, and we just had to add one blue pill and one white pill to our canteen to make it safe to drink. It was the water in the lowlands that I dreaded. When no stream was nearby, we were reduced to taking water from a paddy or a stagnant pool. Although the purification tablets made the water drinkable, nothing could change our thoughts about the possible contents. Overall, though, we never lacked water. Each of us usually carried four canteens, which generally was adequate between fills.

Sending the locations of preplanned artillery concentrations to artillery regimental headquarters each night was a difficult and frustrating task. The concentrations had to be transmitted by radio and in code. Furthermore, from time to time artillery headquarters would send preplanned concentrations of their own to us in code. More than once they sent a whole list of grid coordinate locations in code, in rapid succession, before I could even find my pen and pad and turn on my flashlight. And more than once the Australian artillery regimental commander came on the air to reprimand me and other FOs for not getting it down right the first time.

Though the weather was good during the first part of the operation, the last week was a gloomy, rain-drenched affair. As we moved over the hills and finally down the southern slopes and around the base to the east, it either poured or drizzled constantly, keeping us all soaked. These conditions, plus our not having bathed in weeks, began to cause rashes. Woodie developed a terrible case of crotch rub, and before long he could hardly walk. Brave as he was, he finally asked if I would get him out. On the next helicopter resupply, I had him evacuated back to base camp. His absence presented no real problem for me. I still had my own radio operator, Private First Class Gleason, who was more than capable of handling the job and did so for the rest of Operation Vaucluse.

Back at base camp Captain Eure got wind of my losing one of my radio operators. Without asking, he sent a replacement from A Battery. I wasn't displeased with the replacement: in training he had proved good at handling radio transmissions. But I soon found out that doing well in training and doing well under field conditions were vastly different matters. We had reached the southern base of the hills and were hoochying up for the night when a rifle shot broke the stillness. No one thought much about it, but shots came again and again. Somewhere off in the distance, we concluded, a vc was sniping at us. He never came close to hitting anyone, but just the same the company commander asked me to drop a little artillery in his direction. I proceeded to plot my target. Since the situation was a mild one and my replacement radio operator had never had this kind of "live" experience, I ordered him to raise A Battery on the radio and deliver the initial call for fire based on the information I gave him. In a tighter situation I might have grabbed the radio handset myself, but I thought this would be good experience for him. It didn't work out. The poor kid was so shaken that his attempts to talk on the radio didn't make sense. He was scared to death. Gleason took over and we called in the fire mission, dropped a few rounds in the general vicinity of our sniper, walked the rounds about a little, and then called "end of mission." Our sniper never did shoot again. My replacement operator must have been relieved.

It was here at the southern base of the hills that a European war correspondent joined C Company for the remainder of the operation. I was given responsibility for him, and so for the rest of Vaucluse he and I hoochied up together and spent hours talking. He had just spent several days with the U.S. marines up north, had fallen into an ambush with them, and seemed relieved to be elsewhere. He had no further problems. The few more days of our operation concluded without further contact with Charlie.

We moved to our final extraction lz, and there to no one's surprise found that we would have to chop down bamboo before helicopters could get in. This was typical of the whole operation: landing zones almost always had to be chopped out. Days earlier, when we had to medevac one of our wounded, an area had to be cleared before "dust off" (medevac) could get in. Those pilots had to be admired, landing in holes in the jungle just big enough, blades clipping the edges of uncleared jungle around them. Anyway, clearing another lz on this operation was no new thing for us. While chopping away, I cut up my fingers badly. I had grabbed a big piece of dry bamboo with my left hand and chopped its base with my right, only to have it splinter and explode in my hand, cutting all four fingers deeply. I bled like a stuck hog. Another lesson learned the hard way, not to mention a permanently distinctive set of fingerprints.

When the choppers came in to take us back to base camp, one carried a TV cameraman from one of the major U.S. networks. Since C Company was on one of the last lifts, the cameraman asked if we would mind walking in single file along the edge of the LZ as if we were out on patrol so he could get some film footage. We hammed it up, looking combat ready but about ready to break up in laughter. I suppose we made the 5:00 or 5:30 news. "The Aussies patrol the VC-infested jungles of South Vietnam." What a joke! I wonder how much of what the people back home saw on their TV screens was staged or at least was less than it appeared to be. What a strange climax to a long and physically difficult operation.

Operation Vaucluse, though not spectacular in terms of enemy body count, probably did quite a bit to disrupt enemy operations in the Nui Dinh hills. During the almost three weeks we spent combing the area, we didn't kill more than a dozen, but we did destroy VC observation points, camps, and supplies. And though I think the battalion was disappointed that we hadn't run into the two local force VC companies that were supposed to be in the hills, I was quite content to have survived another month of my tour.

Arriving back at base camp, I wrote home for the first time in weeks. Although in Frances's letter I reported some of the more exciting moments of the operation, to my folks I expressed what were probably my truer feelings. Funny how then it was so easy to write the whole thing off as "boring and hard work," whereas looking back now it seems more like high adventure.

Dear Folks,                                              29 September 66
    Hello once again. We just got back from an operation. The whole thing was rather boring and a lot of hard work. All we did was walk around jungle-covered mountains. We did have some contacts with the VC and lost one of our people in the company (C Company 6RAR).

    I've got a pretty good setup here now. There are four of us in one tent: myself, my radio operator, a New Zealand radio operator, and an Aussie sgt. (a mortar forward observer). Actually, in the field I'm responsible for these people plus two medics and our Vietnamese interpreter. Quite a section I've got, two Americans, three Aussies, one New Zealander, and one Vietnamese. I must say it's an experience. For the first time since I've been in Vietnam I'm fairly well organized and content. Unless we're on operation, I have very little to do except plan arty fires in defense of our company area or in support of small patrols we send out.

After the excitement (or boredom) of Operation Vaucluse, my base camp activities with the company were fairly routine and, except for one patrol, remained that way until the end of my stay with them. I began to settle in and get comfortable. But as usual, my routine was short-lived and my situation soon changed again.

Dear Folks,                                    30 September 66
Just a short note to you today while I have the chance. The days around here are real boring. That's one thing about the infantry, when they're back at base camp, there's just nothing to do. Of course we sent out small night patrols, but that never includes me. I and my section only go out when the whole company goes out because my function is to advise the company commander on the employment of arty fire and the adjustment of it. Since every sgt. and infantry officer must have some knowledge of [adjusting] arty fire, I'm not needed on small patrols. On top of that, it's considered too dangerous to send an FO. The infantry you see, is very careful about protecting their FO because if something happens to him, they might not get arty fire where they want it, when they want it, and as a result, take a lot of casualties. So they watch over their FO like a mother hen watches her chicks.

My dear Frances,                              1 October 66
You said your dad wanted to know how many men there are in the btry and the task force. Actually the total force is about 4,000. There are about 100 men in C Company, of course the number varies depending upon how many people are sick, etc.

In a couple of months now A Btry will be joined by two more batteries of American arty, then forming a new American battalion of arty. I don't know yet whether we'll come under a new battalion name.

I put in a special request today to battalion to be allowed to take R&R during Dec. sometime between the 23d and the 1st of Jan. I hope it does some good.

Well, next week for three days we go out in the bush again on a routine patrol, and then in a couple of weeks another three-day patrol. I think we've got a big operation in Nov. though. That, however, should be my last big operation. We'll get back the middle of Nov. or so, have a month rest or so, and by that time it will be Dec.

3 October 66

I hope you start getting my mail again soon, honey. It must be horrible not getting any; I know I'd feel bad if I didn't get any. I'm afraid, though, that starting day after tomorrow I won't get a chance to write again for three days. Yes, once again out we go on a patrol looking for old Charlie. It's only three days this time, though, so that's not so bad.

Living here at base camp with C Company is quite pleasant. I have one corner of the tent to myself, sort of my little office. I made two desks. One is my arty radio, map, intell. [intelligence] desk, and the other is my regular desk. On it I've got your picture, my new Bulova two-band deluxe eight-transistor table model radio, a fluorescent lamp (powered by batteries, because there's no electricity), and a few other odds and ends. I can get Armed Forces Radio and Vietnamese stations, and when I switch to the shortwave dial, I can get the British Broadcasting System, Radio Peking, Radio Hanoi, and a few others. The last two are especially interesting because they broadcast all Communist propaganda. For example, in our big action here Aug. 18th, they said they killed 300 Australians, or something like that. They're always referring to the U.S. as capitalist, imperialistic warmongers, aggressors in Vietnam, or some bullshit (sorry honey) like that. Of course, then there's Hanoi Hanna in likeness to Tokyo Rose during World War II. Tell Dad about me comparing Hanoi Hanna to Tokyo Rose; he'll get a kick out of it. In every war they seem to have a propaganda reporter like that on the air.

You know honey, I'm not sure at all about me getting to Hawaii sometimes. We'll just have to hope things work out for us, and if not, my homecoming in May will make us that much more thankful.

86

7 October 66

We just got back tonight from a three-day patrol. Nothing happened at all with the exception of finding an old enemy camp. Old Charlie hasn't been too active since he lost 245 men Aug. 18. It's getting late, honey, and I'd better close. Just thought I'd drop you a note and tell you I'm back in.

10 October 66

By the time you get this, my darling, I may or may not be an FO anymore. The New Zealand btry got another officer in sooner than they expected, so now he'll be coming here to Company C, and I'll be going back to 6RAR bn HQ. From there one of three things may happen, (1) I may go out with other companies, (2) I may fly quite a lot, or (3) I may just go back to the btry. At any rate I'll soon know.

11 October 66

Well, tomorrow I'm leaving C Company to go back to battalion HQ 6RAR. I think that my FO job is about over. I'll probably spend a couple of weeks at bn HQ and then go back to the btry. Of course, I may fly a little the next few weeks, but other than that I probably won't do much of anything. Maybe I'll have to go out one more time, but I don't know yet.

You know, sweetie, I really hate to leave C Company. I've made so many good friends here, especially some of the radio operators, the Vietnamese interpreter, and the company commander. I really felt like I was contributing to the war effort. Of course, I will anywhere else too, but here I could see the results and actually be with the men that meet the enemy face to face. I guess I'm over-sentimental or something. I'll bet next May I'll hate to leave Vietnam for some silly reason. I'd probably even extend for another year over here if it weren't for you. I've said many a time, I'm the type of person that doesn't like to leave something once I get used to it even though I don't really like it.

13 October 66

Tomorrow I go to Vung Tau for a few days for R&C. I intend to spend quite a lot of time on the beach and the rest of the time just write letters and go shopping. Of course, I'll sleep a lot.

Well, sweetie, it's late and I'd better hit the sack. I hate to cut it short, but I'll make it up with long letters while I'm on R&C. Good night, my sweetie, for now.

## 7. BATTALION **HQ** 6RAR:
## FO ON CALL

Returning to battalion HQ and the lifestyle there was less than exciting, to say the least. My routine boiled down to pulling shifts in the Tactical Operations Center, eating meals and drinking beer with the battalion staff at the officers' mess, writing letters, looking for something (anything) to do, and worrying about what I might be called on to do next. I was an FO on call, obligated to fill any FO gap that might arise within the battalion. Before a new assignment came up, however, my boss, Major Honner, ordered my section and me to take a few days off in Vung Tau.

My dear wife, 15 October 66

Here I am sitting in a nice comfortable chair with a fan blowing on me here at the officers' BOQ in Vung Tau. These darn guys have sure got it made. Myself and Gleason (my radio operator) spent this morning in the marketplace. The place has a ghastly smell about it and is none too pretty. For example, the fish and meat market: here you see fish, pieces of meat, fat, guts, etc. all just lying around waiting to be bought. They also have huge baskets of snails, crabs, and clams (all live). There's nothing sanitary about all this at all. Dogs and cats are running around stealing pieces of meat, people are sitting around cooking little tidbits of food, Wow! What a horrible smell. Then, too, you see people begging, blind men, crippled people, etc. I saw one poor man without hands or feet dragging himself along the gutter (in water, urine, crap, blood, bits of meat, fish, etc.), holding out his arms for bits of food or money. What a pitiful sight. My God, we must be thankful for what we have, because we're so lucky.

The marketplace takes up about four city blocks, the streets being filled with carts, food stands, clothing stands, all kinds of stands, etc.

15 October 66

Here I am again. This afternoon I haven't done much of any-thing except shoot the bull with PFC Gleason. For about an hour, though, we had a look at some of the bars in town (from the outside). They're all just filled with wenches that lean out the doors and try to pull you in. They say, "hey number one GI, you want number one f--k?" Of course we say, "No want!" Then they come back and say, "You f--king cheap GI, you number 10!" So it goes with us pure GIS. Gleason and myself keep each other straight. PFC Gleason sure is a good guy. You might think he and I get along pretty well for him being a private first class and me an officer. Well if we were in the States, of course, this just wouldn't happen, but in a war zone it's different, especially when one man is with and works for you all the time. You know, you eat together, get shot at together, etc. Of course when we're working our friend-liness is sort of dropped sometimes, but then when we take a break, we're just friends.

Gleason's wife is due to have a baby about the 1st of December. He's beginning to worry a little, I think. He won't know she's even had it or what it is until probably a week after. Isn't that horrible?

I'm really beginning to wonder if we'll be able to get together at Christmas. I'm beginning to get pessimistic about it.

16 October 66

Today's my last day here in Vung Tau. I can't say I really mind though, because I feel like I'm useless and should be getting back to where the war is and be of some help. Funny thing with me, I always feel bad when I take a little vacation because I know there are people back at Baria [Nui Dat] working. I don't think I'll take another one even if the opportunity arises, until my regular R&R comes up.

I hope you all don't send me Christmas presents or anything this year. Just send me a little candy and cookies and lots of Christ-mas cards with lots of letters. A little note from different people would make me a lot happier than gobs and gobs of goodies.

Passes to Vung Tau were welcome breaks from the routine at Nui Dat but were also extremely depressing. There we saw how the support troops spent the war, and I for one resented them tremendously. Though I recognized their absolute necessity and certainly didn't complain about the services they provided, at the same time I envied their "easy life." I can't begin to count the times I scorned them yet in the same moment wished I were one of them.

Dear Folks,                                    19 October 66
Seems funny to hear you talk about frost. Here it's just the opposite. It's getting hotter every day, and the rains come less frequently. We're just about into the beginning of the hot, dry season, which lasts until about March or April. It gets awfully cool at nights, though. Here at 6RAR's base camp it's cooler than A Btry just about 1,000 maybe 2,000, meters away. The reason is because we're in a rubber plantation whereas A Btry's out in the open in a cleared-out banana grove.

Your letters and cookies have been getting here all right. It takes about four days, even for boxes. It sometimes takes me longer to get them, though, because mail, etc., comes to the btry and I have to go over and get it from there.

In about a week and a half I'll be going out in the bush again. We'll be out almost all of Nov., I think. That makes another month that will go by fast.

Dearest Frances,                                21 October 66
Here it is Fri. again and another week almost gone. I think it's the 21st of the month today, but I'm not sure. I'm never sure about the exact date half the time.

Honey, I hope you're getting busy and getting your passport and visa. It may come down to a week before my R&R, and I may still not know where I can go during the time 23d Dec.–3 Jan. Maybe Japan will fall during that time rather than Hawaii; the place makes no difference, just so we can be together. Let's just hope and pray something works out.

23 October 66
This is the third letter I've written in the last few days, and I still haven't mailed one of them. You see, I have to take them to the btry to mail them, and since I have no transportation, it's hard for me to get the letters mailed. I'll get them all mailed today, though. Sure wish I could mail letters every day like I did at Bien Hoa.

The first part of next month I'll be going into the bush again.

We'll be gone for probably three weeks or more. Have I told you this before? I can't remember. So that means me not writing any letters again; however, I'm going to take envelopes and paper out with me this time and try to find time to drop a line even though it may be only a note. You keep up the steady writing, though, because mail will be air-dropped to us by helicopter.

Helicopter pilots have been having bad luck around here lately. Two of the pilots I fly with, when I fly, went down. Luckily one got out without a scratch, and the other is recovering and going back to Australia. I don't know which is safer, flying or foing with the infantry. Both aren't too safe. Even at our btry and at the other btrys (B and C), we've been getting casualties from mines, booby traps, and sniper fire. Let's face it; no job is safe. Even the pencil pushers in Saigon are getting knocked off by vc terrorists. Sure is a rotten war.

25 October 66

Days are going very slow now. Here at bn HQ there's absolutely nothing to do except pull from two to four hrs. duty in the Tactical Operations Center every day and night. Other than that I just sit around reading and working out mathematical puzzles, even a crossword puzzle now and again.

27 October 66

Another night of duty in the TOC. I'm on until 4:00 this morning. I've already had four hrs. sleep before I came on at 2:00, and I'll get three more after I get off for a grand total of seven hrs. This is about what I've been averaging lately sleepwise.

Yesterday as I was going to take a shower; Lt. [Bill] Kingston (my tent mate) grabbed my camera and took a picture of me. I bet it will be real sexy (Ha!).

Lt. Kingston is the [new] assistant bn adjutant for 6RAR. He was a plt. leader in B Company until about three months ago when he had to go to the hospital for an operation. When he got back, someone else had taken his plt., so he was made asst. adj.; also, this would give him time to heal. He's about the best and funniest Aussie officer I've known so far. He's tall and skinny with black hair and plays the guitar very well. He's constantly getting himself in trouble, for example, being too loud in the officers' mess, throwing beer on people in the officers' mess, etc. Of course, he does all this on purpose just to be funny, and everyone just sort of takes all this as a big joke. He's probably the best-liked officer in the bn and a darn good one regardless of his constant attempts to be funny. He takes all kinds of kidding from the other officers. This last week we've (all officers) formed the "I Hate Kingston Club" just to spite him. He loves it. He's constantly imitating how Americans talk, and as a result he's beginning to sound like one. The difference in speech around here between the way I talk, an Aussie talks, and an Englishman talks is always a constant topic of discussion. To me the Aussies sound very English, but there is quite a difference. You'd love the way they talk, honey. Let me just give you some examples of how we speak differently:

| AMERICAN | AUSSIE |
| --- | --- |
| *mom* | *mum* |
| *very good* | *shit hot* |
| *guy* | *bloke* |
| *you damn idiot* | *you bloody idiot* |
| *that's right, I wouldn't kid you* | *fair dingham* [dinkum] |
| *buddy or friend* | *mate* |
| *chicken* | *chook* |
| *girl* | *sheila* or *bird* |
| *beer* | *piss* or *grog* |
| *soda pop* | *goffer* |
| *food* or *chow* | *mucharn* |
| *bed* | *farter* |
| *f--k* | *root* |
| *crap* | *bog* |
| *radio* | *wireless* |
| *record player* | *radiogram* |
| *fellow* | *chap* |
| *shower* or *laundry* | *dobie* |
| GI | *digger* |
| *cup of coffee* or *tea* | *brew* |
| *liquor* | *spirits* |
| *Englishman* | *pommy* |
| lieutenant | leftenant |
| *get the heck out of here* | *piss off* |
| *two weeks* | *fortnight* |
| *rumor* | *furfee* |
| *french fries* | *chips* |
| *all dry breakfast cereals* | *wheaties* |

| | |
|---|---|
| *movies* | *pictures* |
| *small sausages* | *cheerios* |

This is a few of them, just to give you an idea of the language barrier there was at first. I find myself using some of these same terms now.

29 October 66

Just a short note today, sweetie, because we're going out shortly into the bush for a couple of days.

Oh, by the way, we had to put in requests today at the btry for when we wanted to leave Vietnam. The choices were May 1–10, May 10–20, and May 20–30. Of course I put May 1–10. If I could come home the 1st of May, it would cut almost a month off my tour here. Of course, I may come home by ship then and have to spend almost a month on ship again, but that's OK. At least I'll be on my way home to you. It sure would be a thrill coming back into San Francisco harbor under the Golden Gate Bridge that we passed under one year ago.

31 October 66

You may not recognize me if we get together on R&R. Why? Well because I have a great big bushy blond mustache. I've neglected to tell you about it. I started it about a month ago or so. Actually it's really not so big yet, but it's getting bigger. Reaction wanted. Why am I getting so many days off? Well I've had six days now in five months, which isn't very much. The reason is that we're only 30 min. drive away from Vung Tau, and so we all take advantage of it. It's quite a morale boost, you know.

We had some sad news here tonight. One of the guys in A Btry shot another A Btry guy through the head with his rifle. It apparently was *not* an accident, either. The person that did the shooting got himself drunk and just plain shot the other guy. I'm afraid it's a case of murder. The person that was shot just got back to the btry today from R&R in Japan. Isn't that just horrible? He had just called his folks yesterday too from Japan and told them not to worry because things weren't too bad here right now. My sgt. was on R&R with him. He's pretty shook up over it. You just never know what's going to happen. The Lord is the only one that knows, and apparently he knows best. His folks will really take it hard, though, especially because of the nature of it.

Well, my darling, I must close. Until tomorrow.

I didn't get around to writing the next day because my section and I moved to A Company 6RAR for a five-day patrol. We spent a couple of days getting to know them and then headed off into the jungle once again looking for Charlie.

Dearest Frances,                                              7 November 66
Just got back to base camp after being out in the bush for five days. I was out with A Company this time because their regular FO was on R&R. I was more scared on this patrol than I ever have been before because we went so far away from base [camp], the farthest anyone has been away yet. On top of that we went into an area where there was supposed to be a large VC regular force of 300–1,000 men. Needless to say, if we had hit them we would have been in trouble, since a company only has 100 men in it. We did have some action, though. The first night out four VC came down the track to where we were camped. At the last minute they turned around and made off into the scrub. I called in arty fire then to see if I could cut them off. After the second bunch of rounds hit the ground we heard screams, so I guess maybe I got them, although we couldn't find any bodies the next morning. The survivors probably dragged them off. Then on the third day we captured three VC, two women, and about 1,700 lb. of polished rice. That amount of rice would have fed a VC battalion for a while. Also that night we laid an ambush on the trail nearby. About 11:00 P.M. a cart pulled by two bullocks came along; the driver was talking to himself, and we were on one side of the track waiting for him. We had orders to shoot anything that came along and just hope it wasn't women or children. Well we opened up, killed the bullocks, and wounded the man. As soon as we opened up, the man started screaming, "Me no VC, me no VC"; well whether he was or not, we don't know. He died a little later on in the night. Chances are he was VC, because why else would he be pussyfooting around in the dark?

Well, sweetie, if you haven't already noticed by my return address, I'm now a first lieutenant. I became a 1/lt as of Nov. 1, one year and three or four days from the time I reported for active duty in the army at Fort Sill. It doesn't seem like I've been in the army that long, and certainly doesn't seem like I've been a 2/lt. for a year.

I don't know if I told you or not, but one of the 2/lts., a platoon leader from C Company, is being court-martialed. He's a real nice guy but a little bit too much of a kid yet. He just turned 20 a month or so ago. Remember the copter pilot I told you about that got shot down? Well he was only 19. There are a lot of young officers over here, not only in the Aussie army but also our army.

This particular patrol had some pretty scary possibilities. I felt as though we were being sent out as bait in the hope that Charlie would hit in strength, thereby exposing himself to swift retaliation by the battalion. To me it seemed like a planned battle of Long Tan. Fortunately, either we didn't zero in on the right area or the VC didn't take the bait. Charlie usually didn't hit in force unless the chances for success were good or there was no alternative.

The patrol came to an end on the fifth day when we were extracted from the area by helicopter. As usual the choppers were crowded, troops sitting anywhere there was room and holding on to anything stationary. The doors were open as always. Then something happened on board my ship that I'd often worried about. As our helicopter banked, some on board began to slide across the floor toward the open doorway. You couldn't slide far, because people were also sitting in the doorway, on the edge. The danger was that the sliding mass would force some off into thin air. We scrambled and clawed, grabbing one another and anything fastened down inside the chopper itself. Radio operators especially, with the heavy radios fastened to their backs, gave momentum to the sliding. We held on. No one fell out, but we spent the rest of the trip home hanging on. Looking back on this incident now, dangerous as it was, I don't really think it bothered anyone much. In fact, most of us probably forgot it by the time we reached base camp. If one were to ask the people on board that day if they remembered this near disaster, I doubt they would. These things were commonplace and just a part of the many little incidents that occurred daily. The only reason it sticks in my memory, I suppose, is because I had worried beforehand about the possibility. But then I always worried about the little things.

After the excitement of the jungle and being with a rifle company once again, the return to battalion headquarters was welcome, but at the same time I felt a bit let down. I never could seem to make up my mind—I hated the boredom of headquarters life, but I was always relieved to be back in a secure area. I feared infantry operations in the jungle, but I loved being with the men who fought the war and felt that was where I ought to be to make my contribution.

Whatever my confused feelings, I spent the next 13 days back at battalion headquarters worrying about R&R, pulling duty in the TOC, and once again, just waiting for something to happen. And of course I wrote more letters.

Dearest Frances,                                                8 November 66

I don't know if I told you, but I was supposed to go on an island assault operation this week. But since I had to fill in at A Company I missed out on the operation. Maybe it's a good thing, too. Today a couple of helicopters went down with troops aboard. C Company, the company I was with for a couple of months, is also on that operation. I wish I had been with them. I really liked it there. I sometimes think I'll be an FO for the full year. I hope not, but who knows. I'd like to get back to a btry pretty soon, because when I get back to the States, I'm liable to be a BC, and if I am I need the experience in the btry. Oh well, I'm not going to worry about it; I guess I'm fairly content doing what I am. I've made some darn good friends here.

Dear Folks,                                                     9 November 66

I didn't get a chance to see the president [Johnson]. I imagine the only people that did were those at Cam Ranh Bay where he stopped and maybe some administrative people that could take the time off to fly up and see him. Cam Ranh Bay is north of here about 150 miles or so. We stopped there when we were on ship in June. It's a real beautiful place.

Well, I'm glad they're putting some films of Australians and New Zealanders on TV. During our three-week operation on the mountain, there was one TV cameraman there taking movies of our company, C Company 6RAR, on the last day. The films could have been that, I suppose.

Dearest Frances,                                               10 November 66

For some reason yesterday and today have been frustrating days for me. It seems like I go through these periods every so often, especially when I have little else to do but just sit around

96

and think. You know, so far I haven't minded Vietnam, the danger, the firefights, the tensions, my being scared, and the filth. The thing that makes all this so unbearable is not being with you.

I must tell you about something that happened or has been happening. One of my Aussie mates has always been trying to talk me into going to Vung Tau with him sometime and getting drunk and having a woman. Well the reason he's been so insistent, I guess, is because I told him one time that I was so happily married and had such a wonderful wife that I would never ever touch another woman. Being single, I guess he finds it hard to believe in such love, but I've convinced him. Here's what happened: He and another lt. have been going to Vung Tau whenever they can to have a massage and what goes along with it (well, you know). Well, one day I happened to go down too and met them there, and of course they insisted that I go have a massage with them. I refused flatly, but they wouldn't take no for an answer, so they proceeded to try and get me drunk. We drank a long while, and still I said a firm no. Well I finally told them they'd just have to go without me, but I would walk them down there. We went down there, and once more they tried to drag me in. I just absolutely and very violently told them I was not going to do anything against my religion and wife. So that was that. Later on he told me, "You know, it's too bad there aren't more people like you. I really admire you." You can't imagine how good that made me feel. A person will be respected if he sticks to his principles when he's right.

Dear Folks,                                        11 November 66
    Just thought I'd drop a short note to you today while I have the chance. In a week we're going out on a three-week operation again. This should take us well into Dec. One good thing about it, the month of Nov. will slip by fast and hardly be noticed. Then when we get back hopefully I can begin getting ready to take R&R, providing, of course, R&R comes when it's supposed to. Sure hope it does; sure would like to see Frances during that time.

    It's hard to believe it's getting so cold at home. I sure am glad I'll be coming home at the beginning of summer next year rather than winter. At least the climate change won't be so great for me then.

Dearest Frances,                                    12 November 66

It must be nice for those other wives [members of a Vietnam wives' club Frances belonged to] to get all those lovely things from their husbands, tailor-made, etc. from Saigon. Unfortunately your husband can't get to Saigon, because there just happens to be a war going on here. Oh, I can pick up garbage in Vung Tau when I get there, but why waste the money? Let me tell you honey, this stuff they're buying, whether they'll admit it or not, is costing them a fortune. As for furnishing our new home, I wouldn't have Vietnamese garbage or an oriental room in my house for a million dollars.

I guess I'm kind of shooting off at the mouth, aren't I? I know you understand that I'm in a different situation than their husbands are. Maybe I ought to remind you that those people go to work in offices every day, sleep in a room every night, and go out with barmaids every so often because they've got nothing else to do. Your poor husband gets wet, dirty, muddy, sometimes can't take a shower for two or three weeks, most of the time is a little bit scared, gets shot at once in a while, sees dead people, people without heads, without a chest, without legs, arms, brains oozing from a broken skull. And who do you think will tell the biggest war stories when they get home? Of course, those old combat soldiers that bought all these goodies for their wives while in Saigon. Well, anyway, I'll be proud of my year over here. Those bastards deep down will know they didn't really see the war and that they're really full of hot wind. Dad always used to tell me about people like that. If I had my way about it, these sorts of people wouldn't be allowed to wear the ribbons (decorations) that we get here. It's unfair to the combat soldier.

Well, honey, time to close this rather nasty letter. The boredom is getting to me, I guess. You'd be surprised how this damn war affects people. Nerves just go all to heck. It's even happening to me, I think; I get all shaky once in a while for no good reason at all.

13 November 66

It's awfully warm here today, real hot and sticky. I went to church this morning but didn't get much out of it. The padre is a Church of England padre. I guess the reason I don't get much out of his sermons is because I drink beer with him in the officers' mess every so often, and as a result just don't look at him as a minister. It's a perfectly ridiculous outlook on my part.

Our three-week operation begins at the end of this week. It was to begin sooner but was postponed. That means we'll get back sometime during the first week in Dec.

15 November 66

By now I guess you realize that the three-week operation hasn't started yet. It's due now in a couple of days. You asked how far are we going out from base; well, we will be about 14 miles out into the jungle from our base area. Also, during the operation we'll walk another 30–40 miles back and forth in a search and destroy type movement. So we'll walk a total of 50 or so miles through jungle and at no time be any farther out from base than 14 miles. Now this doesn't sound like very much, but when you consider all of this is heavy jungle and that in jungle it takes about one day to move two miles while searching, it's quite a lot. It's the farthest we've ever been out by a long ways. The big battle we had Aug. 18 was only 1½ miles from base camp. You can tell by this that distance from base camp means nothing. In this country 1,000 VC could come within 300 yds. or less of base camp and we'd never know they were there. So distance means nothing as to likely enemy contact; it only means more or less work. Operations, however, are based upon where we think the enemy is.

I found out when I'll be coming home in May, honey. It's official now. I'll be on my way home sometime between the 1st and the 10th of May. The reason some of us get to go earlier is so everyone in the bn doesn't leave at the same time. People in the bn start leaving for home the 1st of May, and the last will leave the 27th, exactly one year from the time we left.

I'll find out whether or not I can get my R&R for the time we want in about a week now.

16 November 66

Well, in another few days the operation will begin. I just found out today I'm not FOing for the infantry directly this time out. Instead I'm FOing for an armored personnel carrier (APC) squadron. So at least I won't be walking much during the next three weeks, I'll be riding. I'm taking my camera on this operation. Cameras are one of the funny things about this war. So many people carry them, from the lowest infantry soldier on up. Of course, half the time a person doesn't have or take the time to take pictures, but occasionally you get a good one.

Tell me, honey, do you tell your folks or anyone what I write you about our operations, contacts, etc. etc.? I'm just wondering if you have and, if so, what they think about it. I sometimes think that a lot of people back home still don't realize there's a real war going on, and thus they probably think that this is just an ordinary tour of overseas duty. There's probably not too many people that think like that, but I'll bet there's a few ignorant people around. Tell me, honey, do most people appreciate our plight, or do they tend to ignore it? I'm just curious, that's all. You know, honey, if anyone ever says it's too bad that Gordon had to go there, etc. etc., you just tell them that there's a job to be done and I'm proud to be doing it for my country, regardless of the hardship it has caused us as a newly married couple. Honestly, though, I suppose if I had had the choice of whether or not to come here, I certainly would not have. On the other hand, if I had been single, I may have volunteered. I don't know.

Well, honey, Thanksgiving this year is going to be rather poor. If we were with an American unit, we would celebrate it anyway. The army provides a real feast, you know, even here; however, since we're not with an American unit and on top of it we'll be in the bush, our Thanksgiving dinner will consist of a can of rations and maybe a hard cracker or chocolate bar. Sounds horrible, doesn't it?

19 November 66

By your letters I guess you think I've been out on operation the last week or so. Well, I'm just going out day after tomorrow. The reason you haven't been getting letters for the last week is because of the five-day patrol I was on. You'll be getting lots of letters for the next week or so, though. I wrote quite a bit between the end of the patrol and now. I'm taking writing paper on the operation with me. I intend to write as much as I can.

Ever since we got to Vietnam everyone has been troubled with rashes. I've never had any, but all of a sudden I've got one. I got it all down my right arm and on my right side. It sure does itch. Also I've got a big sore on my back where a tick dug himself into me. I guess sooner or later a person gets something over here. Both the sore and the rash should clear up, though, within the next week or so. That's the way it usually works.

Happy birthday, honey. I hope this letter gets to you somewhat close to your birthday. It will probably be one or two days late, though. I'm afraid I don't have a card I can send you or my folks for their [25th] anniversary.

My tent mate 2/Lt. Bill Kingston is going home Dec. 11th. His dad has cancer of the stomach and isn't expected to live. He has two young sisters, six and 13. He's in a heck of a situation. He's a regular career army officer, too, so he can't get out of the army, and of course he doesn't want to get out. So because of his situation, the army is transferring him to a station close to his home so that maybe he can keep an eye on things. He sure hates to leave here, leave all of his friends in 6RAR.

I sure hope I can go back to the btry after Xmas. I like it here, but I need experience in something else now. Yesterday our bn cmdr. of 2/35 was at the btry. He said to me, "I guess you've been seeing quite a lot of action, haven't you, probably more than anyone in the bn!" Of course I said I didn't know, and I don't, and that yes we had been in a couple of firefights. That's all he said then. Well, I guess that's sort of an honor, to be the only officer in the bn seeing much action, although I don't really consider myself having seen much.

Myself and my FO section are being recommended for the Bronze Star and/or the Army Commendation medal. Also, I am being awarded the Air [Craft] Crewman Badge and being recommended for the Air Medal. I feel quite honored, although I'm certain someone else must deserve them more.

20 November 66

Well, sweetie, I guess we just saved $1,000. Yes, that's right, I didn't get R&R at the right time. Our hopes went down the drain. What else can I say, honey, things just didn't work out. Well, it will just be so much more wonderful when I come home in May. Only five months and about two weeks, and I'll be home for good.

Well, tomorrow I go out on operation. I'll be kind of glad to get out again for a while. It breaks the monotony of base camp living, anyway.

# 8. OPERATION INGHAM AND MY LAST DAYS WITH 6RAR

The mission of Operation Ingham was to search for and destroy Viet Cong Provincial Battalion D445 and as many of its operational base camps as possible. D445 Battalion had been engaged by 6RAR both in Operation Hobart and in the battle of Long Tan. Both times D445 had suffered. In Hobart they had taken over 30 casualties, and in the battle of Long Tan many more. This operation was supposed to be the final blow to them.

Ingham was different from previous operations for me. Since 161 Battery had all the FOS necessary to support the infantry rifle companies of 6RAR, I wasn't needed. On this operation, however, elements of the Australian 1st APC Squadron, later redesignated A Squadron, 3d Cavalry Regiment, were functioning independently from the infantry as a separate maneuver force. In the past they had for the most part furnished transportation and tactical support for the infantry battalions, but for this operation some elements were acting separately as mobile maneuver forces with missions similar to those of the infantry companies—seek, close with, and destroy. It was more feasible for them to operate in this fashion now that the dry season was beginning. Earlier their mobility was hampered by the wet conditions of the monsoon, but now the tracks were free to operate off the roads and roam the paddies, grassland, and scrub bordering the jungle with little fear of getting stuck in the red mud. With this new kind of mission, 1st APC Squadron made some changes, one of which was to assign a direct support artillery FO to the maneuver element under the command of the squadron commander. Major Honner gave me the job. My function remained the same as it had been for the infantry, but at least this time I rode rather than walked.

The APC squadron consisted of armored personnel carriers,

some outfitted with .50-caliber machine guns and others with twin .30-caliber machine guns mounted in small turrets. Some of the tracks could also house 81-mm mortars. These vehicles with 6RAR mortars aboard accompanied us into the operational area. While part of the squadron hauled the 6RAR infantry into position, our segment of the squadron including the mortar tracks moved into position on the southern tip of the area.

The men of 1st APC Squadron were as different from the other Aussies as the Aussie artillery was from 161 Recce Flight and 6RAR. They were cocky, sure, and had the experience of Long Tan and other actions behind them. They wore black berets, light green jumpsuits, and shoulder holsters for their 9-mm Browning automatic pistols. At least on this operation I could dig out my own shoulder holster and wear it without becoming a laughingstock. In other units, especially the infantry, wearing a shoulder holster was regarded as Hollywood and just plain nonsense. But here among the cavalry, as well as among the pilots, the shoulder holster was the in thing. So I donned mine and played the role, at least for a couple of weeks.

The squadron commander, and my commander for the operation, turned out to be the most professional and impressive officer I'd yet known. He was lean, roman-nosed and very, very British. No wonder he seemed British—he was. He was a graduate of Sandhurst, the British equivalent of West Point, and of the Armour School. Everything was done very properly, he saw to that in his quiet manner. Perhaps it was this manner that impressed me the most, his soft-spoken but authoritative orders given quickly and clearly even in tight situations. Also, he had an almost theatrical flair. Once when we stopped during a rainstorm, he extracted a large black umbrella from somewhere on board our APC and nonchalantly took a stroll among the parked tracks. The guy had class.

Accompanying us for the operation were a Vietnamese sergeant interpreter and two U.S. war correspondents, one of whom was Sean Flynn, son of the great Hollywood movie actor Errol Flynn. The sergeant did little during the whole operation except collect C ration cigarettes from those who didn't smoke, though during the last days he finally did interrogate a couple of Viet Cong suspects. The war correspondents, of course, took a lot of photos and interviewed many of our people. Later they left us and spent a few days with the infantry. The next month an article about their adventure appeared in *Time* magazine giving Sean Flynn credit for saving the Aussie infantry from a Chicom claymore mine. I learned later that Flynn did not survive the war in Vietnam. He, among other correspondents, was listed as missing in action in Southeast Asia.

We in the maneuver element of the APCs departed for Operation Ingham a few days later than 6RAR. They began moving into position 6,000 to 7,000 meters east of base camp on 18 November, and we started our movement and sweep to the south and east on 21 November. We moved due south of Nui Dat for quite a distance, then turned east on a highway that eventually took us 15,000 to 16,000 meters east of Nui Dat and a bit farther south. We were the southernmost element of the entire operation. Our trip was not uneventful. Two or three times we ducked as sniper fire popped overhead. And at least once that I can remember, APCs from our column lurched out across the surrounding paddies in search of the snipers. These were just minor incidents, however, and they slowed our movement very little. One time I even dropped a little artillery on an area we thought the sniping was coming from.

Movement in the APCs was fairly comfortable, though a bit dusty now that the dry season had begun. The rear top hatch of our track was open, and we stood in that open area as we rode—the squadron commander, me, Jim Gleason, my radio operator, and one or two more. Farther ahead, the APC vehicle commander stood in his open hatch manning the .50-caliber machine gun, and to his left and a bit farther forward the driver's head stuck through an open hatch. If necessary, we could close all hatches and "button up," but that cut visibility, so we rode open all the time no matter what was happening. Only at dark, as we lay in our night position, was everything closed up tight.

Riding the APCs was like riding in the back of a truck. As we stood in the hatch opening, weapons at the ready and pointing to the sides, our elbows rested on the top edges of the hatch opening, so upper chest, shoulders, and head were all that was visible above the track profile. This was a fairly safe means of transportation except for rocket-propelled grenades, mines, and accurate small arms fire, yet I think the infantry was safer than we were. Though we had light armor, speed, and a lot of firepower, we were a large target. But during the first days of the operation, at least, Charlie was not tempted except for minor potshots.

Dearest Frances,                    22 November 66

Believe it or not, I'm writing this letter from out on operation. I told you I would. We even got mail today. It sure is good to get mail out here. It means more than at any other time. This is really a boring operation being with the APCs. I'd rather be with the infantry. We have had a couple of contacts even at that.

After reaching our designated area south of the infantry sweep area, we began our patrol and sweep of the paddies and the jungle edge around them. We had little difficulty moving in the paddies. The fields were dry, and the green rice was beginning to turn color. It reminded me of Nebraska wheat fields in late June, a week or so before harvest.

Our patrolling in the jungle was limited. When we did venture in, we moved with great difficulty and in my opinion were quite vulnerable to short-range attack. Because of the danger, on at least one occasion we had infantry with us, ahead, behind, and on our flanks as we pushed through. Our searching was fairly successful. Though we ran into no enemy at this stage, we did find tons of rice, other food supplies, and many camps. The infantry found more of the same, and my old company, C Company 6RAR, found one cache of over 50 tons of polished rice. We spent considerable time just hauling these food stores out into the open paddy where they could be picked up and taken away by helicopter. The bad part was that the VC probably got at least part of their rice back. The word was that the rice would be given to South Vietnamese villagers, but most would be forced to give some of it back to the VC, while others would give it to them voluntarily. The whole captured rice situation was a vicious circle.

While we swept our area of responsibility, 6RAR moved into position north of us and began sweeping down through the jungle toward our location. They ran into several groups of local Viet Cong, VC base camps, and food stores, and unfortunately they began encountering booby traps—claymore mines in particular. Though they killed several Viet Cong, they too suffered casualties. It seemed that the local VC were using delaying tactics while the force we were looking for, D445 Battalion, slipped away.

As always, we plotted our movements and locations carefully on our maps. The key in Vietnam was not just to find the enemy, but also to know where you both were on the map. Without accurate map locations, artillery support, resupply, and tactical air support were difficult, impossible, or in the case of air and artillery fire support, downright suicidal. For transmitting our map locations over the radio nets, the Aussies used a system that precluded encoding map grid coordinates every time we wanted to let someone know where we were. Each day different map grid coordinate line intersections were designated as "city," "cigarette," and so on. To let someone know where you were, you just had to come up on the radio and indicate location by saying, "Kent [Winston, Marlboro, or whatever], left one, down two." This meant that your current location was one grid square (1,000 meters) to the left and two grid squares (2,000 meters) down from the intersection point labeled cigarette.

There were times, however, when this method was not to be used. If, for example, you encountered vc and you transmitted "Contact, vc squad, Winston, left three, up one," you would have compromised the "cigarette" grid intersection. Assuming the vc had been monitoring the radio net (they did have radios, and certainly they knew where they were when the contact was made), it would be a simple matter from the transmission to plot the cigarette map point. Thereafter the vc could plot all locations given from that point on their maps. What we were supposed to do—and we did except for an occasional mistake during the excitement of contact—was to report enemy contact locations, in the clear, by the actual grid coordinate numbers.

At night we always established our night position, our laager as we called it, out in the middle of a large paddy or clear area. This was the same method used in setting up artillery fire support bases and reminded me of the "circle of wagons" American pioneers had used during the westward movement. The thinking was that if Charlie hit, he would have to advance over open flat ground to reach us and thus suffer .50- and .30-caliber machine-gun fire from our tracks as well as the artillery and mortar fire that would be brought down on him. This was a completely valid method, since Charlie used no aircraft in South Vietnam.

The nights spent out in open paddy next to the APCs were pleasurable compared with the nights I spent in the jungle while with the infantry. It rained little, so I generally just put down my air mattress and strung the mosquito net over it without putting up my shelter halves. Many a night I lay there looking up at the stars, trying to pick out the Southern Cross and dreaming of home. It was all so peaceful, even though you never knew whether Charlie was lurking nearby or he was about to dump a few dozen mortar rounds on you, or whether he too lay out there somewhere staring at the stars and thinking the same thoughts of his home and family. Though the time and place were less than desirable for dreaming and reflection, I will never forget those beautiful nights under the stars.

One night a tremendous explosion to my left front shattered the peace of our starlit bedroom. A U.S. Navy ship several thousand meters to the south in the South China Sea, shelling the coastline, made a mistake and hurled one of its huge shells far inland, right to our location. We thought initially that the vc might have lobbed a 120-mm mortar shell, but off in the distance we could hear the naval gunfire. We made an urgent radio call asking the navy to check instruments and firing data. A few more of those shells just a little closer would have meant disaster for all of us. Thankfully, the navy got the message.

Conditions in general were better with the apcs than any I had experienced during my assignment to the Aussies, except for base camp life. We received mail more frequently than the infantry, stayed cleaner, rode everywhere, and didn't have to lug all our equipment on our backs. At times the atmosphere was even conducive to writing letters. I got an official letter from the commander of 161 Recce Flight saying that if awarded the Air Medal, I would be the first one who had flown with them to be so recognized. I felt bad about that: I had flown with them for only two weeks and would probably get a medal. They flew countless hours, but because they had no equivalent award, they would get nothing for their efforts but a pat on the back. That seemed to be the general situation with the Aussies and Kiwis: for them to be decorated or "mentioned in dispatches" the personal achievement had to be fantastic, whereas in our system merely excellent performance might be recognized. The Aussies and Kiwis often joked about the medal-laden American servicemen in Vietnam.

As the days went by we moved farther east and north and thus had to make a major river crossing. The day before the crossing, we reconnoitered and chose a spot to ford. The river here was fairly wide, at least 100 meters in places, with the water swift and deep and the banks steep. Once again I wished I knew how to swim. We found an adequate spot to cross and spent some time practicing.

The next day found us at the river ford in strength. The first APC dipped down into the water and began its trip to the other side. It reached the far shore without incident and with some difficulty climbed the steep grade onto dry land. The second track followed as we, the third APC, waited for it to reach shore before beginning our own descent down the near bank and into the river itself. Just as the APC ahead of us began its climb out of the river and up the opposite bank, a tremendous explosion engulfed one whole side of the vehicle. Then a number of VC took off running along the bank, across the river from us. The first APC to cross took off after them with its .50-caliber machine gun blazing. We made the ford almost immediately after the explosion and as soon as the blasted APC had pulled away from the bank, we also joined the pursuit. It was over quickly. Two VC lay dead on the riverbank, one with his head split open like a broken egg from the mouth up, brain and skull lying spread out on the grass still connected by hair, skin, and flesh. One or two more dead VC floated down the river; the remaining men had disappeared into the jungle. These VC—locals, judging from dress and equipment—would set no more mines.

The APC that had taken the blast of the mine detonated by the VC suffered little damage, and there were no casualties. Instead of detonating beneath the track, the mine blew up along the side and into the air. Fortunately no one on board had been sitting on that side, so the whole affair concluded favorably for us. The VC had probably seen us make our practice runs the previous day, had correctly concluded we would be back, and had placed the mine hoping to disable at least one of our APCs. We were extremely fortunate. Had the VC been not locals and ill trained but rather VC main force or NVA armed with recoilless rifles and RPGS, there would have been hell to pay for all of us that day.

Dearest Frances,                                    26 November 66
How was Thanksgiving? You know what I had for Thanksgiving Day dinner? Well, I had a cup of coffee, a pecan cake roll, and a nice big can of ham and lima beans. Ugh! Well anyway, next year's will be better. I hope we'll be at base camp for Xmas; at least then

we'll have a decent meal, maybe even an Xmas tree. What we'll use for a tree, though, I don't know.

Dear Folks,                                    26 November 66

We've been out for six days now, so thought I'd try and get a letter off. This operation may be making news back home because of our results so far, so you might be watching in the papers. Here I thought being with the APCs this trip would be a piece of cake compared to being with the infantry; however, not so. It's been pretty hair-raising so far. It seems as though nothing's good over here.

Dearest Frances,                              28 November 66

In a short time we'll be back at base camp. Only a few more days now, and we can all take that long-awaited shower and start living like humans again.

We're about to move, so I guess I'd better get ready once again. I've taken four rolls of film so far on this operation. By the way, honey, on one of my films I took a picture that's not too nice to look at. It's a couple of Charlie we had just killed, and one doesn't have much of a head left. I'm sorry if you don't think I should have taken this; take it with a grain of salt and just sort of put it away.

A day or so after the river crossing we proceeded east and high-tailed it full speed up a dirt road. We were to move into an area to the north, adjacent to a rubber plantation and near the forward artillery fire support base being set up by 161 Battery. We had 8,000 to 10,000 meters to travel, and at this point we were concerned that there might be other mines or ambushes along the road ahead. Consequently we moved as fast as possible, hoping to run any ambush or to speed over any command-controlled mine before it could be blown. As we rode, I could practically feel, or at least imagine, mines set to explode in the road beneath us. Then it happened! Over the APC radio net an excited track commander behind us in the column of march reported, "We've hit a bloody mine!" The lead track, our vehicle, and a couple of other APCs had passed over the mine without exploding it, but the next one had hit it. Or maybe it had been detonated by a VC off the side of the road who just happened to select that APC. Luck was still with us, however. The mine, just like the river-crossing mine, had exploded up the side of the vehicle instead of under it, causing no damage to the APC itself. This time, however, we had wounded. Some of the men in the track had been sitting on top near the edge and had caught the explosion and shrapnel as it blew upward.

We continued moving on up the road until we reached what we thought might be a more secure area. As we pulled up into a hasty defensive position, the track that had taken the mine blast moved up next to us. It was one of our 81-mm mortar tracks, and the wounded Australians on board, though not badly injured, were suffering. One was really hurting. In addition to shrapnel wounds to his face, his eardrums were damaged. One of our medics ran up and put drops into his ears, but instead of easing the pain they increased his agony. "Dust Off," the medevac helicopter, finally arrived, and we evacuated our wounded. As evening approached we reached the 161 Battery fire support base and laagered in for the night.

The next morning we began a sweep of the area immediately north of the fire support base. Suddenly .50-caliber machine-gun fire erupted just ahead of us from our lead APC troop. We sped ahead and broke into a small grassy clearing surrounded by heavy bamboo thickets. There our lead troop of several tracks stood dispersed around the edges of the clearing with .50-caliber machine guns pointing silently into the thickets. As they had roared into the clearing, a large number of gray-uniformed Vietnamese carrying cargo packs had jumped up from the grass on all sides of them and run off into the thickets without firing a shot. The troop commander estimated there must have been over a hundred of them. The APC machine gunners were so taken aback at seeing VC flush from all around them that they hadn't fired until most of the gray-clad enemy reached the safety of the bamboo. I immediately checked the map for probable enemy withdrawal routes and radioed 161 Battery, "Hello 42 for ———, fire mission battery, over," using Aussie/New Zealand artillery procedures. In a minute or less the battery was ready, and I was anxious to begin saturating the little valleys and streambeds that ran away from the clearing and thickets with artillery rounds. But we couldn't fire. Clearance as always had to be obtained from higher headquarters before artillery firing could commence, and on this occasion they wouldn't give it to me. An Aussie Special Air Service patrol was somewhere in the area, and HQ, fearing the artillery might fall too close or even on them, refused to let me fire until the SAS location could be pinpointed. Ordinarily, obtaining clearance was no problem, but in this case we were dealing with a commando-type organization that went sneaking about the jungle in small groups searching for the enemy. The problem, so I was told, was that the SAS carried only a Morse code wireless transmitter and therefore could not be reached. Headquarters had to wait for the SAS to call them. Finally, after about half an hour of waiting, they located the SAS patrol and gave me clearance to fire. Though I blasted the suspected withdrawal routes with over a hundred artillery shells, I knew the chances were slim of even coming close to hitting anything. An infantry sweep of the area later proved this out. No evidence was found of the gray-uniformed VC. We had missed a golden opportunity to wreck Charlie's supply system.

The gray-clad VC cargo bearers were a mystery to everyone. No one had ever seen VC wear gray before, let alone what appeared to be gray uniforms. Local VC wore whatever they had, mostly black. D445 Battalion and the Viet Cong main force regiments of Phuoc Tuy Province, 5th Viet Cong Division, didn't wear gray. Not even the North Vietnamese army wore gray as far as we knew. Who were these guys?

After our encounter with the "gray phantoms," we moved westward along a trail toward a deserted village. We saw some movement among the huts and tried to flush whatever it was. We had no luck, however, so I blasted the whole area with artillery fire, hoping to at least make whoever was about uncomfortable. The sweep concluded, we moved back south into the general area of the 161 Battery fire support base for the night.

In the days following other incidents occurred, but generally the operation began winding down. One day we were visited by two or three Aussie generals who flew in by helicopter from task force headquarters. One was the task force commander, and I believe the others were on an inspection visit from Australia. Another time we discovered a small cache of VC stores that included letters, documents, and photographs. The rest of the time we mostly just patrolled, waited around, and provided support and transportation to whoever needed them.

The letters, documents, and photographs proved of some interest. One letter had gone to Hanoi, from there to Paris, France, and had finally arrived in South Vietnam. Whether this was the normal mail route I don't know. One photograph was especially interesting: it showed two men, one in the uniform of the South Vietnamese army and the other in what appeared to be a Viet Cong uniform. I suppose they were brothers. I think the real difficulty of fighting this strange war in South Vietnam struck home the day I saw that picture.

Dearest Frances,                                  4 December 66

We got back yesterday from the operation. This completes Operation Ingham. We didn't quite get done what we wanted to do on this operation; our mission was to find and destroy a vc battalion operating in the area. We knew almost exactly where they were; however, they got away. I think the closest we came was one day when bugles started blowing; that's a means of control by well-organized vc units. At any rate, they didn't feel like fighting this time, so we never found them. We did, however, run into many small groups during the operation, of which we killed 10, wounded 12, and captured one. This isn't really too good for being out for two weeks. We did, however, capture most of old Charlie's rice supply, 80 tons of it, maybe more. All this rice was rice imported from the U.S. [The burlap sacks were stenciled with "NATO U.S. Crop of 1965."] Somehow Charlie got it. Charlie's going to be awfully hungry unless he can get some more rice. He'll probably harvest rice himself now; the harvest season is just beginning here.

All told, we took quite a few casualties during this operation. We had two killed and over 20 wounded, among them (the wounded) the Aussie 2/lt. I used to live with [my battalion HQ tentmate during the pre–Long Tan mortar attack of 17 August]. Actually, we weren't too bad off until our last day of the operation, when we lost 12 people. It will all take a little explaining, so here goes. On our road sweep the last few days we started hitting mines laid for us. As a result, on the last day we couldn't get out of the area because we figured our return route was mined. The infantry helped get us home by clearing the road of mines. One mine [command-detonated claymore] exploded and got 11 men. This is why the Aussie casualties were so heavy. On that last day things were pretty hectic.

One of the sad things of war happened, too, on that last day. Two [Vietnamese] men were along the road when the infantry swept it. Instead of just standing there, they started running, and of course the infantry just naturally took them for vc. They killed one, and he turned out to be unarmed, about 50 years old, and the only schoolteacher for miles around. Such are the breaks of the game. For all we know, though, he may have set some mines. You never know.

The days following the end of Operation Ingham were the last I spent with 6rar. Once again, as was always true between operations, I pulled duty in the battalion hq toc and increased my letter writing. They were sad days, these last ones with 6rar.

Dear Frances,                                           5 December 66
In a couple of days now 161 Btry is going out of direct support of 6rar to be replaced by 101 Btry [Royal Australian Artillery] for the remaining six months of the year. This means, of course, a complete changeover of fos here in 6rar, including myself. We'll all be leaving the infantry now and going back to our respective btrys and let the new fos from 101 Btry take over. My section will move back to the btry on Dec. 15th. There we'll live and work; however, we'll still be on call to go out at a moment's notice with the infantry or someone. Both myself and my section are going to hate to leave now that we finally are. We've lived and fought with them for 4-1/2 months now, and we've all made good friends. You know, I really love the bn, 6rar, just as if it were my own. Unfortunately, I don't have that same feeling about A Btry yet. Maybe I will someday if I'm there long enough. The infantry just has something that the arty can never have, and that's the closeness of everyone for each other. I guess maybe that's because everything's so much more dangerous and everyone trusts everyone else with lives more so than the arty does. Of course arty accounts for a lot of vc dead, but it's hard to realize your accomplishments back at the guns. The fo reports the arty fire that he called in killed so many vc; well that's really no different than hearing a newscast. The fo or infantry, on the other hand, actually sees what he's done. I'm proud to have lived with the infantry.

113

6 December 66

One of our plts. had a good contact last night. They were moving outside our perimeter to set up an ambush for the night when the forward scout heard men talking. They crept up and saw 12 vc in a group eating supper. They crawled to within 20 yds. of them and opened up. They killed five, wounded four, and captured all their ammo, weapons, webbing, and gear. So today is a happy day for all. The plt. was from good old C Company. The big joke this morning was how appetizing the splattered brains of the dead vc looked on the captured equipment. Hell of a joke, isn't it? It's amazing the queer sense of humor one gets after a while. I suppose, though, things like this must be taken lightly, otherwise we'd all go batty. I saw the equipment this morning and it didn't really look very nice.

7 December 66

Eight days from now I'll be leaving good old 6RAR to go back to the btry. It sure will seem different. You know, honey, actual living conditions at the btry are worse than here now. The Aussies have been working hard, and as a result we live pretty good here at base camp. We've got a real nice officers' mess or club as we call it. Oh well, I'll welcome the chance to get back to the btry, though. Of course, even back at the btry I'm still an FO on call if needed.

9 December 66

It amazes me sometimes that I can be so coldhearted over here about death, terror, horrible mangling of human flesh, etc., and yet be so weak when it comes to being separated from you. I just want to get back to my own country and appreciate it for a while. I'm afraid this tour of duty has made me a home lover, and it will be a while before I'll want to leave the U.S. again.

What I just said brings up a point I've never thought of before. This year of war may have changed me somewhat. Perhaps it will make me bitter about some things. I think you'll have to help me sort of grow out of it when I get home.

10 December 66

I sure am tired tonight, honey. Once again I'm sitting here in the TOC as duty officer having one heck of a time staying awake.

I sure wish I knew what the future holds for me jobwise. As you know, I go back to the btry the 15th of this month, however, the new BC, Capt. [Andrew] McGarry, wants to talk to me about going

114

to B Btry as their FO. Well, it's between me and Roy, and I'll do my darnedest to stay here. I've been an FO now for seven months, much longer than average. Of that seven months, ½ month was spent flying and 4½ months with the infantry [and armored cavalry]. The other seven FOs in the battalion can't even come close to that. The bn. cmdr. himself (Lieutenant Colonel Haskell) told me that I was probably seeing more action than anyone else in the bn. I want a job change, not a battery change.

Dear Folks,                                13 December 66

So you were shocked that we didn't have a good Thanksgiving after all that was said about plenty [of] food, etc. over the news. Well, the btry had all this, but you must remember myself and my section are with the Australians and were on operation. Anyway, the Aussies don't celebrate Thanksgiving. Thanksgiving is purely an American holiday. Most of them had never heard of Thanksgiving before. If we had been with an American unit, then we would have had turkey, etc. for dinner even if we had been out on operation; however, since we weren't with an American unit, we just didn't celebrate Thanksgiving.

Another thing, you wondered if helicopters could get to us. Helicopters are used all the time. A whole flight of them will come in, pick up a company, and move it just like that. It only takes 30 seconds to load a company and take off again. You also fly to the attack. Helicopters also bring in supplies and mail every two or three days or, if you're with an American unit, every day. Helicopters mounted with rockets, machine guns, etc. also fly around all the time in the areas of operation. When the helicopters can't land to let off supplies, mail, etc. because of the heavy jungle, they just hover right over the treetops and then drop the stuff down through the trees. The same goes for men; if you can't land, then you have to climb down rope ladders from the helicopters to the ground. You've probably seen pictures of this.

Well in a few days I'll be out on operation again. This time I won't be with the Australians. Myself and also the whole of A Btry will be on operation with an American airborne unit. I'm sure you'll be hearing about this one on the news.

The reason I said you'd hear about this one is because it is an American unit. You've never heard much about the Aussies just because of the fact that they're not an American unit. An American unit made headlines in the *Stars and Stripes* last week for capturing six tons of rice. On our last operation we captured 80 tons of rice and didn't even make the paper at all. That's the way it goes. The same goes for Australian newspapers. They mention all the Aussie actions and say very little about the American forces. Anyway, we'll make news now; oh, you may never hear A Btry or myself, but we'll be with them. I'm sort of happy to get out with an American unit once for a change.

Well, guess I'll close for now. Tomorrow I move back to the btry. This is who we'll be with from now on, unless of course, my section is needed for something.

Certain events and incidents during the months I spent with 6RAR defy chronological placement. For example, at some point between August and December 1966, my section and I participated in at least two patrols or minioperations involving the cordon and search of villages. The specifics of where and when escape my memory, though parts of these operations remain as clear as if they happened yesterday. Then, too, I vaguely recall participating briefly (one day I think) in a joint operation with 5RAR near the southern base of the Nui Dinh hills.

During one cordon and search of a village we had the opportunity or misfortune, however one views it, of working with the South Vietnamese national police and ARVN. Though we spent most of the day just surrounding and sealing off the village while search teams went in, at one stage our group swept through a group of huts. Our movement was soon livened up a bit when the national police and ARVN began shooting up the area to our front. We figured a group of hidden VC had flushed, and we ran forward ready to engage the enemy. It turned out the ARVN and national police were simply shooting chickens and other fowl that were wandering around the village. It was about dinnertime, and I suppose they were hungry. When we asked what all the shooting was about, they replied, "VC chickens; we shoot VC chickens."

During another village search, or perhaps it was the same one, we found ourselves in an area teeming with snails. Since most of the time there was nothing to do but sit around while the search teams went through, we spent our time collecting some of them. Someone suggested we eat them, since in some parts of the world they're considered a delicacy. Never being one to turn down an invitation to eat, I heated a canteen cup of water to boil our exotic lunch. We popped them into the boiling water, shells and all, and let them cook until we figured they were done. The easy part accomplished, we spent the next two hours trying to get them out of the shells. We did manage to extract some, and with a little C ration salt, they found their way into our curious stomachs. They weren't bad at all.

Working and living with 6RAR had been an unusual and interesting experience for my FO team and me. I suspect it had been unusual for the Aussies as well, having three Yanks around. We learned much about them, and I'm certain they learned a lot about us. We had lived with them for almost five months, and at least in my case, they were the best mates I had. I hadn't been around my own battery enough to make close friends there. So leaving 6RAR was a sad occasion for me, though at the same time I welcomed going back to my own unit.

# 9. BACK WITH A BATTERY

Dear Frances,                                             15 December 66

Well, I'm back at the btry now. I really don't have anything to do as of yet; however, I'm beginning the slow, painful process of relearning fire direction procedures and computations. Apparently, I'm at the btry to stay at least for the next couple of months. Roy Minick got transferred rather than me. I'm still on call but who knows, I may never have to go out again, with the infantry, that is.

Our month-long operation over Xmas has been canceled. I can't say I'm disappointed at all. We may go out on some other one within the next month, but it won't be such a long one. At any rate, right now, so far as we know, we're not going anyplace. So I guess I'll go ahead and take my R&R next month anyway. I can't say that I'll have much fun, but at least I'll get away from this for a while.

I'm including a picture in this letter of A Btry officers minus the BC. [Lieutenants] Chuck Heindrichs (executive officer), me (FO), Roy Minick (FO), Doug Mistler (liaison officer) and kneeling, Harry Litchfield (fire direction officer) [Doug and Harry were assigned while I was away with 6RAR]. We're a grim-looking crew, aren't we? Yesterday and today has been the first time in at least five months that all the officers of A Btry have been together at any one time.

20 December 66

I finally got around to writing again, sweetie. I've missed the last three days I think, maybe more. I'm sorry. Life here at the btry is almost like garrison life back in the States. It's a far cry from the infantry.

Like I said earlier, we'll be spending Xmas here and won't be on operation like earlier expected. However, we are going out for a long period of time right after Xmas, early in Jan. This one will last for a month at least, and we'll be moving completely out of Australian territory.

Thank you so much for the Xmas card, honey. I sure will miss you during Christmas. I've been getting lots and lots of cards, all with letters in them. I've even gotten letters from members of my home church. They've been good letters too, very understanding and warm. I guess people do care, even though a person doesn't think so sometimes.

We've got our mess hall all decorated for Xmas now. Nobody really cares except for the two-day truce. Everyone just figures it will be a good time to get drunk.

22 December 66

Three more days and it will be Xmas 1966 in Vietnam. It will probably be my most remembered Xmas and probably my worst. Actually I won't even think of it as Xmas, so it will be just another day except for the fact that we probably won't be shooting. Even at that, though, we'll still have to be alert, truce or no truce. We'll have a big dinner here on Xmas day.

Well, darling, nothing else to write for now, so I'll close. I love you. I hope you have a very merry Xmas.


Being back in A Battery was almost like being transferred to a new unit. Though I'd been assigned there since before we left Fort Carson, the only time I really spent with it was on board ship, the weeks staging at Bien Hoa, and one week in base camp at Nui Dat before I began flying as an aerial observer. I had spent only a little over a month with A Battery in Vietnam compared with 4½ months living and working with the Aussies. It was a big change for me. A whole new war and set of experiences were beginning.

A Battery was different now than before my departure on 1 August. My FO team and I had made it back to the battery from time to time during our duty with the Aussies, but we stayed only a few minutes or an hour at most while we mailed our letters or shot the bull with someone. Now that we were back to stay, the changes seemed striking. Changes in the physical facilities and in personnel, especially the new battery commander, Captain Andrew McGarry, gave A Battery a whole new look and atmosphere. The Fire Direction Center was now a large bunker. Each of the six howitzers was surrounded on three sides by three-foot-wide walls; bunkers had been built next to each of the gun positions and connected to the walls, and in some cases dirt had been shoved up against these walls, making the total thickness five feet or more. Other bunkers stood throughout the battery position, and to our west front—the perimeter—bunkers were built into the four-foot-high earthen berm that separated us from the paddy and jungle. Beyond that lay claymore mines and barbed wire. The whole battery area was much more secure now than five months before.

The FDC bunker was the strongest and most highly developed fortification in the battery area. Initially, walls of sandbags and empty 155-mm powder canisters were laid alongside our tracked and armored FDC vehicle. When the walls reached about seven feet high, the FDC vehicle was pulled out and a roof was put on top. The roof was about three feet thick, made of metal, wood, and layer upon layer of sandbags. The southern end was closed off by conex containers, and they too were sandbagged—sides and top. On the south end from the inside of the bunker, a ladder led up to a small camper trailer shell placed on top of the conex containers, and in front of it a tower extended upward another 10 feet or so. Inside this large bunker was all the fire direction equipment, radios, telephones, our switchboard, and several sleeping areas. It was a structure to be proud of, and the FDC crew was—no question about that.

Outside the FDC bunker and 20 feet or so to the east stood the officers' tent. It was simply a "general purpose" tent without a floor or any of the niceties I had gotten used to in the 6RAR base camp. Here in A Battery the officers lived no better than any of the men, if not worse, a much different state of affairs than among the Aussies. The tent was hot and dirty, and it lay next to the dusty main road that entered the battery area. Oh how often I wished I were back in the relatively cool rubber of 6RAR.

The NCOs and enlisted men had established a club—a tent with bar—and we officers were frequently invited in for a drink. Our own bar, constructed from beer cans, was inside an extra mess tent just west of the FDC bunker that also served as the BC's hooch. We never spent much time there, though once in a while we lieutenants would go over to crack a few beers and talk about college days, fraternity parties, and so on—all those things that were number one to us a little over a year ago but now seemed completely irrelevant.

The new mess hall was the only permanent building in the battery area, and by Nui Dat standards it was beautiful. It was probably 100 feet long by 20 to 30 feet wide, constructed of wood with a concrete floor. Inside were the kitchen area, a large enlisted men's dining area, and a smaller NCO/officers' dining section. There were tables and chairs, and even tablecloths. This was the one place in the whole area that seemed a little civilized and almost made you think you were back in the States. The food was good; we ate off trays, and in the evenings the mess hall served as our movie theater. Before my tour of duty ended, and between operations, we put up two more of these buildings, one as the battery headquarters and supply building, and the other as a large EM/NCO club. Also, concrete-floored tin sleeping hooches for the men were built. The last building erected just before I left Vietnam was the officers' hooch and club. When I left in May I regretted, just a little, not being able to enjoy what it had taken us so long to get.

The battery personnel also seemed different, in some cases because they really were new. Captain Eure was gone, and that alone changed the whole atmosphere. Eure had been funny, overbearing, and loud, and he commanded by his unique personality tempered with years and years of military experience as both an officer and an enlisted man. He got on people's nerves, but nevertheless he was a great BC. All of us disagreed with him at one time or another, but in retrospect he was probably right most of the time. I didn't understand then that a commander has to do what he knows or judges to be right at the moment, despite what anyone else thinks. Captain Eure did his job well, and for most of us, I suspect, he will always hold a special place as the extraordinary man who took us to Vietnam and made us function as a team in combat.

Our new BC, Captain Andrew McGarry, was fairy quiet and reserved, and he commanded A Battery in a more conventional manner than Eure. He used the internal chain of command better than Eure had, and he let us do our jobs without interference or undue harassment. Of course, everyone was experienced now. In the days when Eure commanded, we were all new and green. I've often thought in the years since Vietnam that we could not have had two better BCs; Eure, dynamic individual that he was, driving everyone in those early days, and McGarry, calm, understanding, and gentle, guiding us during our final six months. I have great respect and admiration for both of those fine men, different though they were.

Two of the A Battery officers had gone in the past months, and new ones had arrived. Lieutenant Harold Grace and a temporary assignee had gone home, and replacing them were Lieutenants Doug Mistler and Harry Litchfield, both transferred from other batteries within our battalion. Both were great guys. Doug was one of the kindest people I've ever known, and Harry was very eastern and somewhat serious, but extremely likeable. All of us—Doug, Harry, Chuck, Roy before he left for B Battery, and I—got along famously.

During the time I had been away, A Battery participated in several Aussie operations—Holsworthy, Crownest, Canberra I, Robin, Queenbeyon, Yass, Hayman, Ingham, and Canary. Most of these were small 5RAR or combination 5RAR/6RAR operations that required them to move two or more guns out of the battery base camp and set up at a forward fire support base. In terms of casualties, they had been lucky so far. The mortaring of the task force area on 17 August caused them no injuries, and only one person had been wounded out on operation. The only fatality was the murder in November.

Even though the battery as a whole had not moved from base camp much during the months I was away, by the time I returned they'd already fired 10,000 rounds of 155-mm ammunition. And as the months went by, we fired at increasing rates. By the middle of January 1967 our total was up to 15,000 rounds, and during phase I of Operation Junction City alone we fired over 8,500 rounds. When I left the battery in May 1967, we were well on our way toward the 30,000 mark.

The other batteries of the battalion, B and C, fired even more. They spent most of fall 1966 out on the big operations of the time such as Attleboro. They'd rarely been in their base camp at all but were constantly on the move from one fire support base to another supporting the 1st Infantry Division, the 25th Infantry Division, the 173d Airborne Brigade, and so on. Even as our role in the big operation scheduled for late December and early January was being canceled so we could remain in support of the Aussies, our sister batteries were moving out for Operation Cedar Falls. Because of all their activity, they suffered more casualties than we did as well as firing more rounds.

Being back at A Battery did have its rewards. For example, the attitude of battery personnel toward me seemed different than back in June and July. I think at first they had considered me just another green officer with a bad assignment. But now that FOing was for the most part behind me, they seemed to regard me and my FO section with respect. We were the only ones in the battery who had seen the war firsthand, even though we'd not seen much, and it seemed to me that they looked up to us a little. Staff Sergeant Turner, for example, an old soldier, veteran of World War II and Korea, took great pride in saying to me again and again, "Sir, you and I have been together a long time: I knew you when you were just green. We've come a long way together." Sergeant Turner had been in my first unit at Fort Carson and had been transferred with me to A Battery. We did go back almost a year. He also liked to tell me how my first battery commander at Fort Carson had assigned him to "look after the new officer"—me! Whether this was true I don't know, but Turner's attitude toward me was an example of how the "green lieutenant" suddenly came to be regarded in a different way.

A Battery personnel in the past months had adopted the Aussie bush hat as standard headgear. Captain Eure encouraged this, and when General Westmoreland visited the battery in September, he too voiced his approval of the bush hat as practical and as an outward symbol of our cooperation with our Aussie and New Zealand allies. Visiting brass of lesser rank than Westmoreland, however, were not sold on our headgear. In fact, some even suggested A Battery not wear bush hats at all because they were not American issue and were therefore unauthorized. Technically, I suppose they were correct; but based on General Westmoreland's favorable comments, we continued to wear Aussies bush hats until higher headquarters finally ordered us to get rid of them. Later in the war, as it happened, the U.S. Army issued a form of bush hat, the boonie hat, for GI Vietnam wear.

In preparing myself to assume FDO duties, I spent many hours studying the artillery gunnery manual. Though our FDC crew was probably as proficient in the technicalities of gunnery as was possible, if they did make a mistake the FDO would bear ultimate responsibility for it. As time went on, I found the pressure of firing without error even more nerve-racking than FOing for the infantry. While the consequences of making a mistake as an FO were never mentioned by the Aussies or Kiwis, with American forces it was made quite clear that an error had better not be made. I had observed the same thing before about how the Aussies and Kiwis operated compared with American forces. The Aussies and Kiwis assumed you knew your job, and the negative was never emphasized. But here, as always, there seemed to be the threat, "Do a good job or else!" Perhaps this was not generally true in Vietnam, but from my experience it certainly seemed to be.

The FDO had little to fear in our battery: our FDC crew was top-notch. In fact, under the encouragement, prodding, and leadership of FDC chief Sergeant First Class Hicks, they were downright superior. A good many were college graduates, and all were exceptionally intelligent. They ranged in origin and occupation from Minnesota farm boy to accountant and forester, and in speech from Carolina drawl to sophisticated midwestern business vocabulary. Every one of them was dedicated, hardworking, and loyal. I will never forget those guys—Hicks, Lee, Davis, Albert, Brinker, Schmidtke, Foster, and Larson, to name a few. In the coming months I lived and worked with them day and night and was constantly aware of how much better they knew FDC procedures than I did. In some respects it was humbling, but I always knew I could depend on them. We learned to help one another, and all of us worked together as a team bent on completing our year without a major error. For the most part we succeeded, never making a mistake of any consequence or harming anyone but Charlie.

During the months I had been in Vietnam, I had seen my artillery battalion commander only once since our move from Bien Hoa in July. Since it was the Christmas season, Captain McGarry thought it would be appropriate for him and me to hitch a helicopter ride to Xuan Loc, site of the battalion headquarters base camp, which I had never seen, and attend their Christmas party. A few officers from each of the other batteries would be there as well. We caught a ride, and in half an hour were drinking cold beer at the battalion headquarters officers' club. This was like another war to me. Here things were more comfortable, more like Stateside, and we all sat outside the club on a large concrete patio exchanging stories and experiences of the past six months. I hadn't seen any of them since Bien Hoa, except for the battalion commander, so we all got reacquainted and pleasantly drunk at the same time. It was here that I realized for the first time that the other batteries rather resented A Battery's assignment to the Aussies. They considered our assignment easy compared with theirs. As for me, however, no one in the battalion even came close in experience to the five months I had spent with the Aussie infantry, 161 Recce Flight, and the armored cavalry. Although the attitude toward my battery seemed to be contempt, the attitude toward me personally was considerably different, somewhere between envy and respect. At any rate, it was nice seeing everyone again, and at least for a few hours I forgot there was a war going on.

At the party, I tried to get the battalion commander to say when I would be taken off FO status. I told him it seemed unfair for me, the only married FO in the battalion, to be the only one ever sent out with the infantry. I got no satisfaction. He replied that I was getting experience no one else had, and that as junior first lieutenant in the battalion I could expect no different assignment for quite some time. I would just have to be satisfied with my job for a few months more. As it turned out, however, I FOed for the infantry only twice more.

The first of my last two FO jobs came up immediately after my return from the battalion Christmas party and just before Christmas itself. Company Sergeant Major Harry Pope, former CSM of C Company 6RAR and now CSM of the Australian Reinforcement Unit, asked if I would be interested in accompanying a platoon-size night ambush patrol. The ambush was to be a realistic form of training for a group of new Aussie replacements and would be led by a brand-new replacement Aussie second lieutenant. Out of boredom and perhaps as a favor to CSM Pope, for I had known him briefly when I was with C Company, I volunteered my services and those of my FO section. I was one man short of having a complete FO team, so I accepted a volunteer from the battery. He could operate a radio and wanted to get out of the battery just once and see what it was like with the infantry. I warned him that this was supposed to be just a training exercise, but that if it did turn into the real thing, he might not like it. He insisted he really wanted to come along, so I finally consented.

Though the ambush was an exercise, we decided to set it in an area likely to produce the real thing, at the northern edge of a little village just south of the task force base camp. The village had been searched in the past, but intelligence maintained that a vc squad continued to move in and out, using the village as a base of operations. Intelligence also told us that the vc squad was probably away from the village at this time and that our best chance for ambush would come if we posted ourselves on its northern edge along a trail cutting through a large earthen dike that surrounded it. Although there was some possibility we might catch the vc coming back into the village, I don't think either csm Pope or I really believed it would happen. I'd been asked to come along to provide artillery support just in case. In this war you never knew what to expect.

In late afternoon we moved out, passing through jungle and banana trees south of the iatf perimeter. We crossed the main road that ran through the village and our own base camp in a swift dash, platoon on line and in unison, just north of the village edge. We then moved slowly westward toward the ambush site. We hadn't gone far when the Aussie platoon leader came over and asked if I had a compass. Of course I did, but as he explained, he had forgotten his. Good Lord, an infantry platoon leader without a compass! I let him use mine as he needed to.

We'd moved only a short distance when from the north we heard crashing sounds. All of us hit the dirt and lay as still as possible while the village children drove a herd of cattle through where we lay. Cattle and children passed within a few feet of us, but we weren't seen. After they had gone we moved into our final night positions. The main body of our ambush party took position along the top of the earthen dike that ran along the side of the village and on either side of the trail that cut through it. They faced north and away from the village, expecting the vc squad to come from that direction. To increase our initial killing ability, we set claymore mines in the direction of the expected vc approach. To our rear and 20 to 30 meters away, a squad-size rear guard took position across the trail so that our main ambush party could not be surprised from behind in the unlikely event the vc came from inside the village. In a few minutes we were all set. Now we just had to wait.

But waiting was the worse part—hour after hour. My section and I lay next to the trail on the village side of the dike, below and to the rear of the ambush party's main body. We fought off sleep during those long hours, not able to talk, smoke, or anything. The night was pitch black and moonless, and we couldn't see 10 feet in front of us. I wondered how we would ever see the vc if they did come down the trail. After a wait of several hours, any misgivings I had were answered. I wrote home a few days later and told Frances most of what happened.

Dear Frances,                                    27 December 66
The night before Xmas Eve I volunteered myself and my section to go out with the infantry on an all-night ambush. It's funny, but I'm really bored with life here at the btry. I just want to get out with the infantry where the danger and excitement are. It makes time go faster. Myself and the other two fellas [Gleason, my RTO, and the volunteer] went out with a small group of 27 men and set up an ambush on an old trail that had been used by the vc lately. An ambush isn't too much fun, mainly because you just have to lie there all night quiet as a mouse waiting for the vc to come along, and when they do, just shoot them down without warning. Well, about 2:00 A.M. five vc walked right in among us, and we didn't see them until they were right on us. They came up from behind us; we were looking down the trail the opposite direction. Luckily our rear guard reacted, and we opened up on them from a range of about five feet—yes, five feet. Well you can about imagine the panic. In fact, the vc opened up on us first before we could shoot. Well we started shooting, and finally everything was quiet again. It was so dark we couldn't see anything. We didn't know if we got anything or not; none of us were hurt. We were afraid then that they were sneaking up behind us, so I called in arty to discourage any vc attempts. Anyway nothing happened any more that night, we just lay there alert. Then when it got light at about 7:00 A.M. we had a look around. We had killed two vc. The one body was lying about 10 yds. off to my right front and the other had run a ways before he died. So even though surprised, we killed two out of the five vc. Of course, by this time the truce was already in effect start-

ing at 7:00 A.M. that morning; however, we searched the nearby village anyway. We took the one body and tied it to a pole and took it to the village and displayed him. I think it discourages other people from becoming VC when they see a bloody pulp hanging from a pole. Some way to spend the night prior to Xmas Eve, isn't it? You know, it's funny; when you kill a VC it's just like getting your hunting limit of ducks or pheasants. Everyone's happy, especially the person who thinks he might have been the first one to get a slug into the VC. Most of us don't think of VC as humans; they're just something to hunt and kill. Funny how a person can become this way, but I guess you have to in order to keep sane.

There was a bit more to the story that I didn't mention to Frances. Actually, all hell had broken loose just as I started to doze off. Next thing I knew, the whole rear guard erupted in rifle and machine-gun fire, tracers going every which way. Some in the main ambush party above us on the dike also cut loose. My section and I put our noses in the dirt and lay flat; we were in the crossfire. Apparently the VC squad we expected to come into the village was already there and was now moving down the trail on its way out. A machine gunner in the rear guard was on his knees urinating when he noticed the VC on the trail next to him. Before he could shoot they shot, and then the whole rear guard opened up blindly. It was a mad, mad minute or two.

When the firing finally stopped, my section and I scrambled up the dike and in among the main ambush party. We called back and forth to see if everyone was all right. The platoon leader got on the radio and called for mortar illumination. The illumination rounds floating down made an eerie howling gobble as they lit up the trail and fell nearby. Checking my map, I picked what I thought might be the VC withdrawal route as well as a possible attack route and called in artillery fire from 161 Battery.

The VC we killed were locals. They were dressed in black, wore shower thongs, carried American .30-caliber M2 carbines, and had little in the way of equipment. These VC were in sharp contrast to the uniformed, Chicom-armed, Ho Chi Minh sandal–wearing enemy we had encountered in the battle of Long Tan four months before. And though I didn't tell Frances in my letter of the 27th, farther to the north and west lay three more VC killed by the artillery fire.

The new Aussie replacements were elated over our night's work. Later, when we were picked up and carried back to base camp by truck, we rode singing and cheering, never once reflecting that we had killed five human beings just 24 hours before Christmas Eve. As for me, I was no different from the rest of them. Like everyone else, I could hardly wait to get back to base camp and strut around, a successful warrior back from battle. As for the young soldier who volunteered to accompany me on the ambush, the one who wanted to see what the real war was like, this was more than enough experience. When I asked him later if he would like to go on another ambush, he replied in no uncertain terms that he was content to stay in the battery area from now on.

Dear Folks,                                    27 December 66
Tonight I'm duty officer in the FDC. Since there are four of us lts. in the btry, we only pull duty officer every four nights, which isn't too bad.

Sorry to disappoint you on your theory, Dad, about why I've been an FO all this time, but the fact is I'm the junior officer in the battalion, so naturally I get the worst job [Dad's theory was that I was the best officer]. Of course, that's a matter of opinion. It may be the most dangerous job, but it certainly is the most satisfying. You'd be surprised how the rest of the people in the btry look up to you as a person who has really seen the war. Of course they wouldn't trade places with me, though.

Now since I'm at the btry I don't have to go out with the infantry unless they call for me. The chances of them doing that are pretty slim. So I just sit here at the btry all the time now. You can't imagine how bad I feel, though, knowing that the infantry's out there fighting and here I sit. Funny about that, but I feel more like I'm contributing to the war when I'm out with the infantry. My radio operator feels the same way. Even though we don't really like to be out in the jungle, yet we feel we should be.

At 7:05 A.M. on the 26th of Dec., five min. after the truce ended, we started things off with a bang. All five arty btrys in the area [1ATF] opened up at once. Then about an hour later a VC battalion was sighted, so we fired on them. We killed 43. In the confusion the VC also lost over 100 weapons. Pretty good for just a couple hours after the truce ended, I'd say.

Dearest Frances,                                    31 December 66

It sure is hot today, must be around 100°. It makes for a very strange New Year. Tonight I'm duty officer, so I'll be spending my New Year's Eve in the fire direction center.

1 January 1967

I never did finish this letter yesterday, so here I am on the first day of the new year, with a hangover [I had partied after my FDC shift, the night of the 31st]. Boy, do the Aussies party. By day after tomorrow things should be back to normal again, I hope at least until Feb., when there will be a four-day truce, the Vietnamese New Year.

Well, honey, everyone here is now beginning to consider himself a short timer. Now we're the old pros just waiting to get out.

Happy New Year, my wonderful wife. I love you.

3 January 67

Another boring day today. Once again, today it was cloudy and rainy. This is all very strange, because for the last couple of months it's been so hot and dry. Maybe this is the winter monsoon. The real monsoon begins again in April or May. At night it's been really getting chilly. Last night it was down to 60°.

Tomorrow night Martha Raye is going to be in Vung Tau. We're sending 20 people from the btry down to see her show. I don't know if I'll go or not. Maybe I will if I can get out of being duty officer that night.

The Xmas goodies have finally stopped coming. Good Lord, I couldn't even begin to eat one-tenth of it all. Most of it got moldy on me, so I had to throw it out. I couldn't give it to anyone either, because everyone got so much. I even got a package of goodies from a 65-year-old woman (old maid) from North Carolina. I wrote her a nice thank-you note, and she wrote back thanking me for writing. I can't possibly attempt to write everyone back home that I got goodies from, so I'm not writing anyone. Just thank everyone for me; that should be sufficient.

Dear Folks,                                    5 January 67

Orders are starting to come in as to when we leave here and where we will get stationed. Some lts. were lucky and are going home as early as April 13th. Two of the officers in our btry are like that. Most of them are getting sent to Fort Sill to be instructors or part of the school support troops. My orders will probably come in as to when I leave and where I'll be going about the end of Feb. As it stands right now, I'll be coming home sometime in May; however, some officers will not come home until June. It all depends on whether or not your replacement is on the way or how soon you have to report to your new unit. I'm still hoping for May.

We haven't been shooting much at all lately. Everything down here is sort of at a standstill. Rumor has it that we may move from here and become a part of the 1st Inf. Div. In a way I hope so. I sure would like to serve within an American div. over here. Of course, if we moved it would mean having to build up another area all over again. But so what, we might as well work our butts off while we're here. Of course, there's only one problem; the Australians don't want us to leave, and the Aussie general has told American generals just that.

The 9th Inf. Div. has been landing just south of us for the last few weeks now. I think they've got one more brigade to land, and they'll all be here. Just before them a separate light infantry brigade also landed (not a part of the 9th). The number of troops just keeps going up and up.

Dearest Frances,                                        9 January 67

The contrasts of this war will never cease to amaze me. Night before last I was on another ambush all night, very real, dangerous, and warlike. Then last night I spent watching TV over channel 11, a Saigon TV station. I felt just like I was home. What a funny war.

Dear Folks,                                              11 January 67

Happy birthday, Mom! Bet you thought I'd forget, didn't you? Well guess I am a little late aren't I? I hope you had a happy birthday. Sometime before I leave here I intend to get you all some little thing from here, so as to make up for all the birthdays and Xmas presents I missed giving all of you. I'm getting a three-day pass to Vung Tau the 17th, 18th, and 19th of this month, so maybe I can pick up some things then.

Tomorrow A Btry is having a very distinguished guest. Premier Ky is coming to visit an Aussie btry, the New Zealand btry, and us. Should really be something.

Dear Frances,                                    12 January 67

This morning was quite a morning. We had quite a visitor in our area. Premier Ky, the top dog (president) of [South] Vietnam, was here to see A Btry. My gosh, were there a lot of news reporters, photographers, etc. etc., plus personal bodyguards, and air cover being flown overhead by the Vietnamese air force. Quite a day! All the officers were introduced and talked with the premier.

One thing I forgot to tell you about that first ambush I went on the 23d of Dec. Remember I told you I called in arty; well I killed three VC with that. I suppose you don't find this very exciting do you? Guess no one can unless you're here. A person is trained to kill over here, and when you do you know you've really done your job.

                                                16 January 67

Brrr, is it cold this morning. It's 60° again. Boy, this weather is hard to take. It gets up to 90° to 100° during the day, and then at night it drops to 55° to 60°. Right now I sleep with a sheet and two blankets. I would have never believed this about Vietnam a couple of months ago when the nights were even hot.

Well, sweetie, this month is half gone already. That means I have about a maximum of 120 days left after this month or a minimum of about 90 days after this month. It really amazes me that we have been separated for eight long months already. When I get home, I'll bet that this will have seemed the fastest year of my life. It will seem just like this year never happened. You know, this darn country is beginning to seem like home, like I've always been here.

                                                19 January 67

Here I am in Vung Tau on my three-day pass. I have to go back the day after tomorrow. Another officer from our bn is on pass with me. He is quite the guy. He'll probably get the clap (VD). Sorry about that! Oh! Oh! guess what? He just walked in with a girl. Will finish later.

I'm back again sweetie. I just left the room. Apparently she's going to be there all night. That ought to be good. Well, I'll give them an hour or so, and then I'll come back and go to bed and try and sleep. Sounds hard to believe, doesn't it? Well such is life in Vietnam. No modesty, morals, or anything. I hope it's dark when I walk into my room. I sure would hate to walk in on them.

Well, honey, I'll close for now. I'll write tomorrow and tell you how this mess came out. It ought to be good for a laugh.

21 January 67

I got back to A Btry today at 4:30 P.M. Actually, I was glad to get back. I just don't care for Vung Tau.

Now to finish telling you about how everything came out the other night. Well, I came back into the room later on and shut off the lights, undressed, and crawled into my bed trying to be as inconspicuous as possible. All the time I could hear them murmuring. Believe it or not, I went right to sleep, and by the time I woke up in the morning, the girl was gone. So anyway things didn't come out so bad. Sure was an ungodly situation, though.

23 January 67

Once again it's rumored that we're supposed to go out on a big operation. This time I think it may come off. If so, we probably won't get back here until the end of March. I'll really be short by then, about 57 days at the absolute most. Remember I said about a month ago that we were to go on a big operation? Well as you know, we didn't. That operation was Cedar Falls, which is still going on. I imagine you've heard and read a lot about it. Well this next one is bigger yet. Everyone really wants to go bad, myself included. Just once we want to go out with American units. If we do go, I won't be doing any FOing, I'll be with the btry.

27 January 67

It's been three or four days since I've last written. I intended to write last night so it could go out in the mail this morning, but something else came up last night. The minute I walked into FDC things began to happen around here, and consequently we were put on 100% alert and fired about 200 arty shells in an hour at a large group of VC. So, honey, I just didn't get it done last night.

I leave for R&R in Japan on the 10th of Feb. I'll spend two days picking up orders, etc. and will actually leave Vietnam for Japan on the 12th of Feb. I'll be in Japan until the 16th or possibly the 18th and then fly back to Vietnam. By the time I get inprocessed once again it will probably be the 20th. I should get back to A Btry that day. I'll probably call you from Japan. Oh, by the way, send me the telephone number, I've forgotten it.

You say your dad was surprised how smart the enemy is with regard to tunnels. Well, believe me they are a very smart, formidable enemy most of the time. There are three different types of them: 1, the local VC guerrillas; 2, main force VC; and 3, the North Vietnamese army. 1 sometimes isn't too smart but still is pretty good because of his knowledge of the surroundings; 2 and 3 are darn good, every bit as good as we are, with just as good equipment if not better. The Chinese and Russian weapons they use are in some cases very superior to ours. We have all of these types 1, 2, and 3 here. Of course, as you go farther north you have more of 3; 2 and 3 all have fatigues (green), carry backpacks, webbing, the newest weapons, 60-mm, 81-mm, 82-mm, and 120-mm mortars, heavy and light recoilless rifles, and wear helmets sometimes. When they attack, they sometimes blow bugles to control their movements. They have radios for communication. They use booby traps, antitank mines, and use every type hand grenade conceivable. Of course, up north they use jet planes that are every bit as good as ours, but their pilots aren't so well trained. They use missiles against our planes. So you see our enemy is smart, well equipped, and well trained. They're losing the war because of our air and arty superiority over them. Of course, the helicopter is the big factor of their defeats. You might mention things like this to people back home, because I don't think they realize that we're fighting against real soldiers, not just guerrillas. This war is bigger than Korea was manpower-wise, though we are not suffering quite as many dead and wounded. The reasons for this are the type of war (jungle), evac. of wounded by copter, and better medical facilities. Also, they aren't using tanks, jets, and heavy arty against us (ground troops) like the Reds did in Korea. You know honey, I'll bet I'll get impatient sometimes when I get home because people just won't know what's going on.

It's really amazing how things are changing over here. Higher HQ keeps trying to push all these stateside things on us. They just don't want to realize that there's a war on. Of course, this war is changing. We're winning, building, and just naturally everything is changing. It's hard to believe just here in the btry how much we've built up. By the time I come home this area will be pretty darn good and secured. This is happening all over in the country. Little by little we're overcoming the VC.

Well, my darling, how was all that for a lecture. I sure wish you, folks, etc. would ask more questions. There are so many things I take for granted, but you just don't know about them. What a job it's going to be someday trying to sort out all my letters, etc. and try to put everything down into one large diary and at the same time add to [it] and draw conclusions, etc. This is something I definitely want to do, though. Get it all arranged, perfected, and then typed and put in book form, for private use only. If I ever could accomplish this, I might even like to make a couple copies and maybe give one to the folks and your folks. It would give them an idea what a year is like over here, or at least what it was like for me. How's that for an idea, honey? A pretty good description of my year, I think, is contained in my letters to you and should be a good basis for a year's running description of events.

Dear Folks,            29 January 67

This btry area sure is changing fast now. We've got buildings up now for all the troops. The officers are still living in a tent with a dirt floor, though. We come last, according to our BC. After the enlisted men's club and NCOS' club are built, then we'll build our BOQ. Our buildings are not very good by Stateside standards, but for here they're pretty good. They're all made out of corrugated tin and two-by-fours, with concrete floors. Actually, they're like big cattle sheds. It's quite a contrast now from what it was when we first got here.

Dearest Frances,            2 February 67

Today the poop sheet came out on when officers go home. Of course, this sheet is subject to change; however, it's the best thing anyone has to go on. It is probably pretty accurate. According to the sheet I leave Vietnam on the 10th of May, which means I should be home on the 11th U.S. time. That leaves me 97 days left in this year's tour.

           8 February 67

I haven't written for the last couple of days because I've been under the weather a little. I've had a bad cough and have just generally felt crappy. It's partly because it's so dry and dusty here, I think. That cold, wet weather in Japan will probably do me some good.

Thanks for the Valentine. I'll try to call you on Valentine's Day from Japan.

Two days after writing this letter I left A Battery for R&R in Japan. I had little idea beforehand just how much was involved in getting there. First I had to catch a helicopter ride from Nui Dat to Long Binh. There I spent a day or so completing paperwork of one kind or another. Then on about 11 February, Service Battery transported me to Saigon's Tan Son Nhut Airport, where I spent another day, mostly just waiting. Finally after a one-night stay at Tan Son Nhut, we donned our khakis, exchanged our military payment certificates for real American greenbacks, and made our way toward the waiting airliner.

We boarded the plane and in a few minutes taxied down the runway and cleared the field. What a liberating experience to be airborne and headed away from Vietnam. At that moment, I remember wondering what it would be like to make the flight away from Vietnam forever. I also remember the sickening thought that in just a few days I'd be coming back. As we climbed skyward, the sight of round-eyed stewardesses surprised me. Then as we leveled off for our straight shot to Japan, a movie began playing on the overhead screens: I watched the whole movie yet really didn't see it. In what seemed no time, we touched down in Japan.

Those few days of R&R in Japan stand out in my mind as the one truly happy period of my whole year away from home. I was completely without worry or responsibility and did only what I pleased, when I pleased. As I wrote Frances in a letter from there, It was as though a thousand-pound weight had been lifted from my shoulders.

R&R ended all too soon for me, as I suspect it did for most of us. There were a lot of gloomy faces on the plane the night we flew back. Whereas during the trip to Japan everyone had been happy and talkative, now our faces betrayed our returning fear, and few had much to say. Perhaps it was the night flight, but I don't think so. I bet that others besides me wondered if we'd survive our final days in Vietnam. I've often wondered how many on that R&R flight died in the following days and months. I'm sure some did, because as we returned the biggest operation of the war was just getting under way. Without even the chance to relish the last six very pleasurable days, many would be thrust into the unknown of War Zone C for Operation Junction City.

# 10. OPERATION JUNCTION CITY

Dearest Frances,                                    19 February 67

I got back today [from R&R]. We arrived back in Saigon at about 7:30 A.M. this morning. I got to Service Btry at Bien Hoa at about 10:00 A.M. and discovered that the whole of A Btry was there. They convoyed up there last night [on their way to War Zone C and Operation Junction City]. Yes, the big operation has finally happened. A Btry has almost moved out of the Australian Task Force lock, stock, and barrel. So tonight I'm here at the btry position [at Nui Dat] packing. I'll catch a copter tomorrow morning and get back with the btry. The btry will come back home sooner or later, but it may not be while I'm still in Vietnam. We expect to be out for at least three weeks, and very likely over two months. So by the time I come back here, it will just be to pack to come home. Boy, what a state of confusion. All I can tell you now about the operation is that it's a long ways northwest of here, and we'll be working with a couple of American infantry divisions. I'm sure you'll read all about it. Just look for a big operation.

The last two weeks have really been hard on morale. Just before I went on R&R some of my very good Aussie friends at 6 RAR were hurt and killed. One sgt. was killed, and three very good officer friends were wounded. Then while I was gone [on R&R], three more officers were killed. One was an FO from the New Zealand btry. I knew him real well. Poor guy had only eight more days left in Vietnam. He had a wife and three kids. I just can't believe it. He had just telegrammed his wife the night before exactly when he'd be home, on what plane, times, etc. Boy, that's hard to take. A person's never safe whether you've got 365 days or one day left. The Lord knows best, but darn that's bad. I just feel so bad about it.

Dear Folks,                                          20 February 67

I got back from Japan yesterday, and now today I'm trying to get to A Btry. When I got back to the btry position yesterday, they were gone. They're on a big operation with a couple of American infantry divisions way up northwest from where we were. So we're no longer with the Aussies and probably won't get back there until the end of April. So now I'm catching helicopters and trying to get up to the operational area. I should get there by tomorrow. Time will really go fast now. By the time we get back from this operation, I'll have not too much more than a week left [to serve in Vietnam]. We'll never be able to enjoy the buildings we built back at base camp. They're just all sitting there empty now. Someone will get some use out of them, I suppose. Hopefully just before everyone goes home we'll go back so we have a chance to pack. All of us had to leave most of our possessions behind. We took only what we could carry and what we need. So once again it's live in mud, dirt, and sand. But anyway, like I said, time will go fast.

You asked what my work is now. Well it's still FOing, but I don't go out anymore. Since I've done so much of it already, another officer will go out instead of me from now on, unless of course they need more than one FO from our btry. So what I'm doing now is fire direction officer on certain shifts. You see, an FDO must be on duty 24 hrs. a day, so we have to pull shifts.

I've got to close for now and catch that helicopter to the forward area. Mail will get to me OK, and I'll be able to write. This isn't like going out with the infantry, you know. Things will be a little better.


Dearest Frances,                                     20 February 67

I'm still not with A Btry. I'm at bn [headquarters] at Xuan Loc right now. Hopefully, by tonight or tomorrow I'll be with the btry again.

Honey, about R&R. After talking to some people that did meet their wives, I'm glad we didn't. They said it was much harder parting the second time than the first. I know you feel bad, but believe me it was for the best, I think. I'll be home for good shortly, God willing.


Operation Junction City wasn't a complete surprise. We'd been alerted several times for big American operations, but because of Australian intervention (I think), our role was always canceled. In

January we missed Operation Cedar Falls, but many of us felt then that if another big operation came up, we'd probably go. Even though Junction City was kept reasonably secret, it had been rumored, and most of us hoped we'd be included this time. The boredom of base camp life, especially in January, had gotten to us. Just once before leaving Vietnam, we wanted to support a big American operation.

The way Junction City began for me was discouraging. I had anticipated returning to Nui Dat after R&R and having some time to box up things I had brought back with me from Japan, send them home, and then ease myself back into the routine. No such luck! A Battery was already on its way to northern Tay Ninh Province, and they needed me pronto. So I hurried back to Nui Dat to pack and then hitchhiked by helicopter to join A Battery in the field.

Getting to A Battery took a couple of days. I caught a ride into Xuan Loc, site of our battalion headquarters, but couldn't make another connection there to get to A Battery. After waiting a day, I finally managed to catch a helicopter ride to Tay Ninh and later another to the forward fire support base of A Battery.

I'd never been in Tay Ninh Province before, and as we landed in Tay Ninh City I was immediately struck by two things. One was the immense number of helicopters parked everywhere, and the other was the sight of Nui Ba Den, Black Virgin Mountain as it was called, just to the northeast, sticking up out of the flatlands as if nature had made a mistake. I didn't have much time to consider these things, however, because in no time we took off again, heading north toward A Battery's location near the Cambodian border, in the Elephant Ear portion of War Zone C.

A Battery's fire support base location was the worst I'd seen. Crammed into a little jungle clearing with it was a battery of eight-inch howitzers and 175-mm guns, an artillery battalion headquarters, its headquarters battery, some engineers, some infantry, a few APCs, and for perimeter guard, several 2½-ton trucks with quad 50 machine guns mounted in the back. What made the position so bad was its size. Our FDC vehicle, for example, stood no farther than 20 meters from the jungle's edge. Not only that, but some of our howitzers were about as close. This presented two problems. First, since the trees were so tall and so close around us, our firing was limited to elevations above the tallest of them. We had to be extremely careful not to fire at lower elevations or we'd have shells hitting treetops and exploding in our own area. Second, the danger of ground attack by the VC against artillery bases was high. The 9th VC Division had a host of regiments in this area, we were told, and if they decided to hit us, there was no open ground around us to give us an opportunity to stop them. Had they hit, I'm sure we would have been overrun in short order, and fighting would have boiled down to individual effort, bunker by bunker and foxhole by foxhole. Even the quad 50s were 20 meters or less from the jungle's edge. A massive ground assault against our position would have been disastrous for us all. Fortunately, the VC in the area either didn't recognize our vulnerability or chose to ignore us, waiting for a better opportunity. Other artillery fire support bases in the operational area were not so lucky.

Though few of us were aware of it at the time, Operation Junction City was designed to search out and destroy the Central Office of South Vietnam and the Viet Cong and North Vietnamese army installations and forces of the area. The latter part of the mission was standard, but we didn't know about COSVN. In fact, during the early days of the operation almost all the information we got came from Armed Forces Radio and the *Stars and Stripes* newspaper. The first overall map of the operational area I saw was printed in *Stars and Stripes*. If the total picture of the operation was ever disseminated to the troops, it missed us. We did know one thing, however; it was big, bigger than any so far, with 20 or so infantry battalions and half as many or more artillery battalions involved. And of course we knew that we were in support of the 25th Infantry Division, whose mission was to seal off a portion of the area and attack into the horseshoelike search area. The whole thing really got under way on 22 February with a combat paratrooper assault made by elements of the 173d Airborne Brigade, the first assault of its kind since the Korean War.

D day was earthshaking in our area, as I'm sure it was in all other fire support bases the morning of 22 February. According to plan and at specific times, we and the other artillery units in our fire support base, and those in other fire support bases as well, fired concentrations around and on helicopter and paratroop landing zones within the operational area. Shortly afterward we began to get reports of how the air assaults and paratrooper landings were progressing. Most of these reports, however, were unofficial or pure rumor. One of the first rumors we heard was that an FO with the 173d Airborne had been shot through the head and killed immediately on landing. We heard other stories equally disturbing, but for the most part the first day of the operation brought little contact with the enemy.

Dearest Frances,                              26 February 67

Well, this is the first chance I've had to write in almost a week now. Hope you haven't worried. We're a part of the biggest operation of the war; however, I doubt if you've heard too much about it, because it has not proved too successful so far. Of course, we don't know for sure. We have to listen to Armed Forces Radio to find out what's happening; we don't find out anything here. That's typical of a large operation. Nobody knows what's happening except a few cols. and generals. Back with the Aussies we knew what was happening all the time. Not so here at all. Here we're just 120 men out of 30,000 involved in this operation. Just as a point of interest, we're located no more than a few miles from the Cambodian border. We don't know how long we'll be here, could be one day or two weeks. Then after that I think we're going to the 1st Infantry Division. Right now we're with the 25th Infantry Division.

1 March 67

Another few days gone, and we're still out here in the middle of nowhere. The btry had to furnish a ground FO for this operation, but I didn't have to go. The BC figures I've done enough of that, so he sent out Lt. Mistler. He's with the South Vietnamese marines. However, it really doesn't make much difference now. It's just as dangerous here in the btry. Two nights ago we were mortared here pretty heavily. We [the fire support base] lost 14 men—13 wounded and one dead. Before this, in the btry, they only had had one wounded and one dead the whole time (nine months). I guess it had to happen sooner or later. So as you can guess, things are pretty hairy down here. The operation as a whole, though, is pretty much a flop. They just can't seem to find Charlie.

So what am I doing? Well, I'm FDO half of the time. Harry and I split it 50–50. We average about four to five hours of sleep a night and no more. The pressure is really on. You see, the problem is, if we make the slightest mistake here in the FDC, arty is liable to land on friendly troops. Even though someone else may make the mistake in FDC, the officer is still responsible. So you have to check, double-check, triple-check everything and hope like heck your men are careful. For a mistake made by one of his men an officer can get court-martialed [or more likely relieved of his duties and officially reprimanded]. So you see what kind of responsibility Harry and I have got hanging over us. There's been a good many arty officers go down the drain this way in war.

The days of the operation dragged on and on. It was hot, dry, and dusty. Each time we fired, and we fired a lot both day and night, our guns kicked up huge clouds of dust. After a few rounds fired in succession, the whole battery area disappeared in the swirling dust, making it difficult to breathe and almost impossible to see. Harry and I pulled shifts day after day and night after night in the FDC, supervising the computation of firing data for both live fire missions and harassment and interdiction fires at night. Our biggest headache was checking and double-checking "no fire zones" that changed periodically, areas that could not be fired into because of friendly patrols, and so on. Then, too, there were our own listening post and perimeter guard field phone lines to monitor. After doing this hour after hour, day and night, 12 hours on and 12 hours off, exhaustion set in and morale began to decline. In the end, I guess, we all patted ourselves on the back. Of the almost 9,000 rounds we fired during Junction City, not one error that we know of was made.

The night of 27 February, the first mortars came. I was off duty and trying to sleep, and in fact I think I had fallen asleep despite the noise of our guns firing H&Is, when suddenly the roar seemed different. I rolled over on my cot down inside my four-foot-deep sleeping bunker, and as I did so I could see flashes in the battery area through the top firing slit. There was no question in my mind what was happening. I rolled off the cot onto the bunker floor, grabbing for my helmet, flak vest, ammo pouches, and rifle as I fell. My big fear was massive ground assault, which sometimes followed heavy mortaring of a fire support base. As the explosions died down, I could hear people yelling. I cautiously emerged from my bunker and walked down a slit trench toward the FDC vehicle.

142

The rear door was closed; Harry had buttoned up tight. Then the casualties began to gather, congregating at the FDC, some walking and others being helped or carried. Our motor sergeant, one of the first casualties to arrive, looked bad. Blood ran from his face and neck, drenching his T-shirt and the top of his fatigue pants. It looked like one of his eyes was damaged. Despite his obvious pain, he stood next to the FDC track supported by others, breathing hard but in control of himself.

In addition to losing our motor sergeant, we lost part of his section (the maintenance section) as well. One 82-mm Chicom mortar round had found its mark and dropped through the entrance of their sleeping bunker. It was a miracle they weren't all dead. All told, we suffered just a few wounded, but the unit next to us in the fire support base had one dead and many more wounded.

Within minutes we fired counter mortar fire, hoping to catch the VC as they, in all probability, headed back across the Cambodian border to safety. Soon after, casualties were medevaced and we resumed firing H&IS. The schedule of fires had to be kept, and since the VC had not followed the mortaring with a ground assault, we returned to our routine duties of the night. The excitement over, I went back to my sleeping bunker and caught a few more hours of shut-eye before relieving Harry in the FDC.

Dear Folks,                                      1 March 67

We've been out for over a week now, and we don't have the slightest idea when we'll be going back to base camp. I don't think we ever will. We'll just go from one area of operation to the next; thus we'll never be able to have any comforts of home. From now on it's move, dig in, move, and dig in. Of course, we're still hoping we may go back to the Aussies, but I doubt it. The American army has their hooks into us now and probably won't let us go.

Dearest Frances,                                 1 March 67

I just got my orders [for home]. I leave here the 10th [of May] or about that. So I'll probably leave the btry base camp on the 8th. If we're on operation out someplace, I'll probably leave earlier, like about the 4th or 5th. Guess where we're going? Ft. Sill, Oklahoma. What I'll be doing there I don't know. It could be in a regular unit (I hope as btry cmdr.) or as a gunnery instructor. Lt. Mistler (Doug) is also going there, plus most of the other officers in the battalion. It will be like a 35th reunion.

You'll never guess what just happened. Just as I was writing the last sentence, we got gas in our area (apparently tear gas). Boy, did those gas masks go on fast. We don't know where it came from. We just found out what the gas was. Friendly infantry was guiding in a copter and threw a gas grenade rather than a smoke grenade.

3 March 67 4:30 A.M.

I'm afraid your husband is pretty tired about now, so this won't be a very long letter. I got three of your letters today; mail doesn't get out here too fast. It takes at least a week or more. I imagine it will take at least as long for mine.

As I said before, Doug Mistler is out FOing now for the btry. He's using my radio operator, Gleason. I am sure glad he's out instead of me now. He's been out with the South Vietnamese marines, also a pleasure which I wouldn't care to have. Actually, though, the darn mortar attack we had here was more dangerous than the week he spent with the marines. You sure never know over here what's going to happen. You just sort of roll with the punches.

The other day we had a man accidentally killed in our area when another guy's rifle accidentally went off. Then two days ago a friendly arty shell went off overhead and sent metal flying around this area; no one was hurt, though. Harry had one piece hit next to his feet. Poor guy has only got 40 days left. Doug Mistler has only 43 days left, and he's FOing for the first time. Back at base camp all of us were feeling pretty short, but now 70, 40, 20 [days] or one day is too much. It's a long drag yet to the end. One of the other FOs in the bn was wounded the other day too. He might lose an eye and one of his testicles. On top of that, a gun from C Btry blew up yesterday wounding five people, plus one of our trucks hit a mine wounding three more. Things are pretty hairy these days.

After the first mortar attack, casualties slowly continued to mount. Some I wrote home about and others I didn't. We lost our first sergeant one night. I was FDO the night it happened, buttoned up in the FDC track and occupied with our usual tasks, when suddenly an explosion crashed right outside. A couple of minutes passed and then someone tapped on the FDC vehicle door. We opened up and there stood the first sergeant, his fatigue pants torn

144

and his leg oozing blood from a small wound. He looked inside in an almost bashful way and said, "I think I've been hit." He had been walking around the battery area, making his final nightly round, and as he approached the FDC track a mortar round exploded out of nowhere, wounding him in the leg. We took him over to the aid station, where they dressed his wound. Since the wound wasn't serious, medevac wasn't called in until the next morning.

Next day, as the first sergeant waited to be medevaced, he limped around the battery area using a stick as a cane, enjoying the whole situation immensely. Around his neck hung a big "wounded" tag, and as he limped around, giving the troops he saw both hell and encouragement as usual, he puffed on an enormous cigar he had gotten from someone in honor of the whole occasion. First Sergeant Francis made the most of the whole affair.

Nighttime was nerve-racking in this area. In addition to blasts of enemy or off-course friendly mortar shells, friendly artillery screaming overhead, and our own H&I firing, we suffered little probes on our perimeter. They didn't amount to anything, but they did keep us jumping. One night while I was on duty, reports of movement on our perimeter from listening and machine-gun posts became frequent. One machine-gun post in particular kept up a steady stream of alarming reports all night long. The guy kept reporting movement to his front and requesting permission to fire his M60 machine gun. Yet when I questioned him over the field telephone, he never seemed really certain he had seen anything. The poor kid was scared to death, and though I didn't let on, I was too. I talked and talked to him, trying to get him to hold his fire until he was certain of a target. Perhaps I should have let him fire. It would have been consistent with the American procedure of shooting at anything that seemed suspicious. But Australian-taught caution prevailed. I refused to let him fire and expose his position unless he was sure of a target. He never did fire, and we made it through the night without a major incident.

Dearest Frances,                                                5 March 67
    Twelve days of the operation gone, and only 56 days more of it to go, so we think. It certainly is a long one. Needless to say, we're ready to go back right now and just sort of cool it at our base camp the rest of the time.

Darn it, honey, I've got to cut this short; we just got word we're moving to a new, more secure position. I guess that's good. By the way, my first Air Medal has come through. Also, the BC has sent in a recommendation for another Bronze Star.

5 March 67 evening

Well, in typical army fashion we've just now got the word no move until tomorrow. Of course, this came after we had our bunkers torn down, bedrolls packed, etc. etc. Oh well, I guess there's not much else to do other than work, so what the heck.

By the way, we just got the hint of a rumor that we may go back to base camp on the 15th of this month. Boy, I sure do hope so. Like I said before, I sure would like to cool it back there until May 10th. Now I still have to get my port call. That's your actual orders with the date you actually get on that plane to go home. Hopefully it will be slightly before the 10th of May. From the 10th [of March] I have 66 days left; that's nine weeks and three days. Just think, honey, by the time you read this letter, it may only be eight weeks and three days. Oh, I hope and pray that time goes fast.

I requested 15 days leave when I get home. In addition to this I'll get about three days travel time. Of course, two of that will be used getting from here to home. It's about an 18 hr. trip from here to San Francisco. From there I'll grab the first 707 to Omaha, another 2½ hrs., and just like that we'll be together again. I should be home then by the 12th and have to report at Fort Sill on the 27th of May, the exact day I left you one year ago.

10 March 67

Since I last wrote we've moved to a new position. We're sitting in the middle of a big paddy field along with many other arty units providing arty support to all who need it. The night before we got here they were mortared, so as a result once again we're well dug in. Every one of us lives underground in holes and bunkers that we've dug and built. It sure is a lot of work. The night before we left the other position we took three more wounded, one of which was our 1st sgt. This came from a friendly mortar shell and a friendly arty shell that mistakenly hit us. This is one of the problems of an arty FDO. That particular FDO will probably get court-martialed [or relieved] for it. Boy, what pressure this is. With the Aussies it isn't bad because there aren't many friendly troops around, but here the operation is so big that any mistake is disastrous.

It's almost been confirmed now that we'll be going back to the Aussies in a couple of days. They've asked for us to come back for one of their operations. It will take us about 18 hrs. to convoy back to 1ATF (1st Australian Task Force). We'll spend about one day there and then move out on an Aussie operation. We won't mind that a bit, though. We'd much rather work for the Aussies than Americans, because we don't have to put up with bullshit from higher HQ there.

Our second fire support base position was much better than the first. At least 100 to 200 meters of open paddy lay around us, separating our position from the jungle. With us were other artillery units, like ourselves firing in support of the 25th Division and the 11th Armored Cavalry Regiment, a few APCs, a few infantrymen, and several Dusters on the perimeter. The Dusters, twin 40-mm guns mounted on a light tank chassis, were awesome weapons. At night during an occasional "mad minute," a time when many on the perimeter just sort of cut loose with fire, the twin 40s would ring the jungle edge with explosive shells. They fired rapidly, the two barrels firing a split second apart, creating a sound much like World War II pom-pom guns on board ships. What an awful but reassuring sound they made as their 40-mm shells screamed into the air and exploded in rapid succession back and forth across the tree line.

In addition to our H&I firing at night and the firing of the Dusters, H&Is were also fired by people on the perimeter armed with M79 grenade launchers. This was a new experience for me. The Australians emphasized more discipline in exposing positions, but out here with Americans the philosophy was prevention. I suppose both methods had their merits, but more than once the dull thuds of M79s being fired from the perimeter into the jungle almost sent me to my bunker thinking mortars were incoming.

Dearest Frances,                                    12 March 67 1:40 A.M.

Another day almost finished. I go off duty at 3:30 A.M. and then hopefully I'll get seven hours sleep until about 11:00 tomorrow morning. Boy, does this get tiring after a while. Up until today things hadn't been too exciting, but today one of the units we're supporting ran into something. By the time you get this letter you will have read about it in the paper or else heard it on TV. It involved the 11th Armored Cavalry.

We had a few more mortars again tonight, but none landed near us. Everything has been pretty quiet around here.

We spent most of our time in the second position supporting the 11th Armored Cavalry Regiment. While sweeping the Vietnamese-Cambodian border in the Elephant Ear sector one day, they made contact with a well dug-in enemy force. The 11th ACR tried to punch in, but the VC held their position and fought them off with small arms, automatic weapons, and recoilless rifles. The Cavalry radio net was busy, to say the least. The 11th ACR commander, directing the attack from his command helicopter overhead, raised hell, bullied, and even personally directed our artillery fire. At one point he observed several APCs stopped and wanted to know why they weren't advancing. The reply from down below was that an APC driver had been hit in the head and knocked cold by an M79 grenade (which hadn't exploded) and they were trying to get squared away. The 11th ACR commander raised more hell. Despite his urging, they couldn't crack the VC position, at least not before nightfall. The next morning they overran the position only to discover the VC had bugged out. No wonder Charlie had stood and fought: the area contained large underground concrete bunkers, and in one of them were a couple of big printing presses. I imagine they were being used to print materials of one kind or the other for COSVN. Also, Charlie had left almost 30 dead in the area. How many of them A Battery was responsible for was impossible to tell, but as far as our gun crews were concerned, the count was 30 kills for A Battery. It kept up morale.

Dear Folks,                                        13 March 67
My first letter to you in many days, isn't it? Sorry I can't keep up, but if we're not busy, we're trying to catch up on sleep. We're all getting pretty darn tired of this and are, of course, ready to head back to base camp. When that will happen, though, I don't know. We could go back tomorrow, and then again we may not go back for quite a while yet. I suppose Frances may have told you what operation I'm on. It's Junction City. It's been a hot, miserable operation all the way, and a costly one for us. We've been mortared two times and had friendly artillery dropped on us twice. The btry had

148

just been too lucky. My god, I'll be thankful to get out of it all in 58 more days. The trouble with this darn war is it's so unpredictable and nerve-racking. Boy, will I be glad to get home.

One afternoon we thought we might be in for what artillerymen dread most, a ground assault by the enemy. An artillery fire support base, out of our range, had almost been overrun a few days before, so when an air observer sighted a vc force just across the clearing in the jungle to our front, we thought this was it for us. We fired at them using the lowest propellant charge possible at practically the highest angle of fire, dropping our shells into the jungle from above. It was the best we could do without leveling the howitzer tubes and using direct fire. The vc, however, were too far back in the jungle for direct fire to do any good. In the high-angle, low-charge mode, our shells left the tubes like rocks from a slingshot. You could actually see those hundred-pound shells arc through the air. We stopped firing as jet planes arrived to bomb the whole area to our front and off into the jungle with napalm. It must have done the trick. We never were hit by ground attack.

The middle of March saw our role in Junction City near an end. We and elements of the 11th Armored Cavalry were ordered to return to Phuoc Tuy Province and participate in a large joint American and Australian operation planned for late March and early April. Most of us were more than ready to go, and as phase 2 of Junction City developed for the artillery, it was none too soon. A few days before we left, a fire support base at Prek Klok was attacked by a vc force. Then just a few days after our departure two others, one at Suoi Tre and the other at Ap Bau Bang, came under tremendous ground assaults from enemy regiments. In the last two engagements alone over 800 of the enemy were killed, but not before portions of the fire support bases had been penetrated and overrun. Junction City was about to come alive with all kinds of action, but luck was with A Battery. We were about to leave.

Dearest Frances,                                    14 March 67
    Tomorrow we leave here to go back to the Aussies. We'll be back one day and then we leave again for an Australian operation. You see, our guns have to move even when the Aussies go on operation. So that means another two to three weeks out in the

bush. Of course, the btry will just sit in one spot the whole time, just like we did on Junction City. Of course, we did have to move once during this one. A good thing too, because yesterday a convoy got ambushed from our old position. That's right, just as soon as we left Charlie moved in. I guess he was probably pretty near while we were there too. We figured he was, and we were awfully glad to get out. It will take us about 18 hrs. to convoy back home from here. Just think, it will take us as long to get back (200 miles) as it will take me to get home come May.

We began our move out of War Zone C on 15 March. The plan was to travel south-southeast to Tay Ninh, then down Highway 22 to Go Dau Ha, east-southeast on Highway 1 past Cu Chi to Saigon, northeast from Saigon to Long Binh and Bien Hoa, east on Highway 1 to Xuan Loc, and finally south on Highway 2 to Nui Dat. The territory we were to convoy through was not at all secure except for the stretch between Saigon and Long Binh. I had missed the convoy A Battery made to Junction City on 18 and 19 February and I kept wishing I could miss the return trip as well. Convoying in Vietnam was not pleasant.

Our convoy home was the largest I had seen. As we pulled into position with the 11th Armored Cavalry and others, we joined a line of vehicles that seemed without beginning or end. Initially we had to make our run down roads cut through the jungles of northern Tay Ninh Province, but as we broke out into the open flatlands and could see in front and in back of us we realized we were part of a line of vehicles of all kinds that stretched for miles. Sometimes we moved at full speed, and other times we crept along. The dry season and the travel of hundreds of vehicles had turned the roads to powder, and as we drove the dust clouds we raised sometimes blinded us. I think we must each have had five pounds of dirt sticking to us by the time we reached Long Binh.

Dearest Frances,                                    17 March 67
       The btry is almost home. Right now we're here in Long Binh (right outside Bien Hoa) at Service Btry of our battalion. We've spent the last day and a half here just relaxing and getting our equipment in shape for the final leg of our journey back to base camp. We've got about 40 miles to go yet.
       Our trip two nights ago from War Zone C and Operation Junc-

tion City to here was not too good. Just outside of Cu Chi we ran into a mortar attack. Then the column behind us started getting recoilless rifle and small arms fire. The column ahead of us also got small arms fire. So we just stopped and waited it out. Eventually all clear was given, and we started off again. We hadn't gone 200 yds. when the last vehicle in our btry column hit a land mine. It blew the vehicle up and wounded four of our people. Lt. Mistler (Doug) was one of them. They're all OK, though. They just got shook up and cut up a little. They'll be back at the btry within a week. Of course, they all get Purple Hearts. That made 10 wounded we've had in the btry since the operation started last month. If I'd counted wounded people that were with us but not a part of the btry, the total is 16. It's been a bad operation for the btry. It's also been bad for the whole bn. You see, our whole bn (2/35 Arty) was out on this operation. B Btry was mortared the other night too, and C Btry has also taken casualties. The total for the bn during the last 30 days is 31 wounded and three killed. Heck, that's equal to what *some* infantry units have, and arty isn't supposed to have as many casualties as infantry. However, that's the nature of this darn war. Everyone suffers alike sometimes. Statisticswise our Bn took 6% casualties this operation (that's a conservative figure).

I know that by writing you about this you're going to worry that much more, but believe me, honey, you're not the only one that's worried. All of us are really counting days now, hoping we can make the few remaining. You pray and I'll pray, and that's all we can do. The Lord knows what's best, and let's not forget that.

At Service Battery in Long Binh we just lay around; some got haircuts, and we all took baths, our first in weeks. We fueled the vehicles, pulled maintenance, and prepared for the final leg of our journey. Someone suggested that we officers might as well go eat at one of the big officers' messes. We walked over, went in, and paid for our food. From the stares we got from those Long Binh combat soldiers, I gathered that they didn't approve of our appearance. All we had to wear was our dirty fatigues, and we hadn't bothered to polish our boots. Somehow it didn't seem necessary. We did our job and did it pretty well. That's all we cared about.

After a couple of days' rest, we moved out of Long Binh, past

Bien Hoa, and east on Highway 1 to Xuan Loc. We were still being escorted by the 11th Armored Cavalry because the route between Bien Hoa and Xuan Loc was so unpredictable. Time and again units were ambushed along that stretch of road: vc main force regiments made life interesting around there. This time, thank goodness, we passed through the area unmolested.

We spent a day in Xuan Loc awaiting further cavalry escort and then finally on 20 March moved out for home. This last leg of our convoy didn't go well for our escort. They attempted to clear the road of mines with detectors, but they missed a few. Once, as we moved along, one of the lead tanks hit a mine and lost a track. Though we lost none of our vehicles that day, the 11th ACR lost several getting us back to Nui Dat.

Not far north of Nui Dat, we passed through a little village completely empty of young men. Only women, children, and old men stood watching as we drove through. At the edge of the village along the road lay a body, and farther on stood a group of South Vietnamese soldiers. It looked as though they were conducting a little operation in the area and had flushed and killed a vc, probably a village resident. The absence of young men in the village perhaps was significant.

A short time later we entered familiar territory, and in less than an hour Nui Dat was in view. Though our base camp was a far cry from Long Binh or even Xuan Loc, it was home, and all of us were happy to be back. Nui Dat meant a shower, a mess hall meal, greetings from our Aussie and New Zealand friends—"How you been Mates?"—and one night of relative quiet. Unfortunately, the following morning we moved out again, this time for Operation Portsea, my final mission of the year.

# 11. OPERATION PORTSEA

Dearest Frances,                                          24 March 67

Once again it's been a while since I've last written. We got back to base camp the afternoon of the 20th [from Operation Junction City], and the morning of the 21st we moved out again for another month-long operation. So here we are again out in the bush. We probably won't get back until the middle of April. This time we're on a large operation of combined forces, Aussies and Americans. You may or may not read about this one. It's called Operation Portsea. Operation Junction City is still going on, but of course we were pulled out early so we could go on this one. This one is in our area of operation. Don't worry about my safety while out in the bush, honey; it's not too safe in base camp either. Last night base camp [at Nui Dat] was mortared. Good thing we weren't there. So you see, no matter where you are, there's no certainty of safety.

Operation Portsea was a fairly large operation conducted east of Nui Dat, and it covered the ground we had searched during Operation Ingham plus an area south to Highway 23 and south from there down to the sea. The old Ingham operational area was being swept by elements of the U.S. 9th Infantry Division, the area just north of Highway 23 by the 11th Armored Cavalry Regiment, and that south of Highway 23 by 6RAR and elements of 5RAR. Though Portsea was mostly a search and destroy operation, the second part of it during April was geared to protecting U.S. and Aussie engineers working on Highway 23. Our mission was mainly to support Australian units, and most of our firing during Portsea was for them.

The search and destroy phase of Portsea didn't accomplish much. A couple of times 6RAR came close to a major encounter with the VC, but except for brief clashes the VC didn't seem to want to fight. A couple of contacts were made with elements of the 5th VC Division and the 275th VC main force regiment. Another time we fired quite a few rounds in support of a 6RAR company that hit a well dug-in VC force, but the VC broke off the encounter, leaving few dead. The rest of the contacts were limited to small, local VC groups. Overall, we didn't do a lot of firing. The operation was a far cry from Junction City.

The fire support base that we shared with one Aussie artillery battery and a mortar platoon was just south of the area where we had encountered mines on Operation Ingham. The route we took to get there was practically the same as I had taken in November and December with the Aussie APCs, and needless to say I feared the trip. With just over 40 days left in country, surviving my tour in Vietnam was something I thought about more than ever.

Our position was in a big open area just south of a rather prominent hill sticking up above the surrounding scrub jungle, grassland, and bamboo thickets. Above us on the bamboo-covered hill, the Aussie mortar platoon and artillery battery labored building bunkers and other defensive positions. The area all around us was open ground for the most part, and just to our east the engineers had put up a substantial barbed-wire fence. The position wasn't bad at all, and based on our experience during Junction City we worked hard to make it even better, spending every nonfiring minute digging in and building sleeping and fighting bunkers. All of us were too short—too close to leaving—not to make the position as secure as possible.

Other than our firing, absolutely nothing happened during Portsea. We were all happy enough about that, but a terrible boredom set in. So we created excitement. Someone in one of the gun sections caught a scorpion and a tarantula and proposed pitting them against each other in a fight to the finish. He put the two creatures in a small box, and a bunch of us gathered around to see the battle. Meanwhile a helicopter flew in bearing a brigadier general from II Field Force in Long Binh. We scattered to our posts, pretending to be busy as the general walked around inspecting our position. We never completed our creature competition.

Our little game was not our first contact with Vietnam's wild creatures. Earlier in the year we had killed a couple of cobras at base camp. We had played around with tarantulas on Operation

Junction City; Nui Dat hill at base camp teemed with monkeys, peacocks, and wild boars, some said; and during this operation we killed another cobra. Our most interesting encounter with animals, however, had occurred early in the year when a U.S. Air Force forward air controller directed the fire of our battery at a herd of elephants. When the mission first came over the radio we joked about it, but as we fired the FAC started taking ground fire. Apparently the elephants were being used by the VC to carry supplies and equipment. The elephant train security force, not caring much for our artillery fire and their principal adversary the FAC, flying overhead, opened up on him with automatic weapons. The FAC reported that he was being fired at by a heavy machine gun mounted on an aerial tripod. What a strange war!

We had just gotten the battery position secured and our bunkers built when Australian artillery headquarters directed us to move to the top of the nearby hill and set up there. The Aussie artillery battery had moved out, and now there was room for us in their old position. It was the same thing all over again—dig holes, fill sandbags, and build more bunkers. The most frustrating thing about leaving a position was having to destroy the old bunkers. Standard procedure was to tear everything down, empty or rip up the filled sandbags, and fill in the holes. We never left anything we thought Charlie could use against us.

Moving to a new position became less of an ordeal as we grew more experienced. Beginning with Junction City, we made it a practice to carry bunker construction materials with us—steel stakes, timbers, poles, and PSP. Perforated steel plank, commonly called PSP by the military, was an item that got tremendous usage in Vietnam in ways other than its primary purpose. Though it was designed mainly for constructing airstrip runways, everyone found it ideal for building bunkers and other structures. At least when you arrived at a new position you didn't have to hunt up material for bunker tops. Carrying all that on our vehicles gave us the appearance of a really junky outfit. Of course everyone else looked the same; besides, the emphasis was on survival and doing the job, not on looking good.

Throughout the year in Vietnam, one of the things that kept me going was letters from home. Every day I looked forward to mail call like a child waiting for a Christmas present. Even if I didn't get a letter, there was still the anticipation of getting one the next day. The letters were especially important during Operation Portsea because of the extreme boredom, but what I read in one letter made me blow my stack, and I wrote back in language I had never before used with my folks.

Dear Folks,                                          27 March 67

Boy, did I get mad today when I read your letter about how someone asked you, "Does Gordon have to carry a gun?" What dumb ass asked that question? My God, I could have screamed when I read that. Why, so help me, if anyone ever puts a stupid-assed question like that to me when I get home, that is, someone that should know better, I'll verbally tear them a new asshole. Sorry about the language, but man, am I mad. Good Lord, just in the last few weeks during Junction City our own btry lost 10 people, not even counting the wounded we had during the mortar attack that didn't belong to our unit but were with us. That would add another six wounded and two killed. On top of that, in the last few months several of my Aussie and New Zealand friends have been killed and wounded. Do I carry a gun? I myself am responsible for dead vc. Well by golly, I'd like to stuff that down someone's throat and see if they still ask if I carry a gun or if Frances was coming to Vietnam. I almost find it hard to believe that people can be that dumb. Now that U.S. casualties are being reported by numbers maybe they'll realize, and how about all those vc mortar and human wave attacks lately? They're even using arty up north now.

Well, we just got a fire mission, so I'll have to close. Sorry this has been such an angry letter, but the business of "Does Gordon carry a gun?" hit me wrong.

Dearest Frances,                                     30 March 67

One of my few and far between letters is once again being written. I think I've become tired of writing. It's just getting so close to getting home that it's hard to write anymore. However, try to keep your letters up, honey, and I'll do my best too.

Nothing much has been happening. We're still out in the bush. We have two weeks to go yet, we think, although there is the possibility of it being cut short, we hope. Harry left the bush today for base camp. I'm FDO now, and he won't be coming back because he goes home in less than two weeks. Doug also leaves in less than two weeks. That will leave only two of the original A Btry officers, myself and Chuck (Lt. Heindrichs): 41 days left for me. At the end of April my job will be all but finished, and the last week I'll just putter around getting ready to go home. We should be getting two new replacement officers in the btry within the next two weeks, and of course my replacement about the end of April. We just got two new FDC EMS in the other day. I'd hate to be them. They hear all of us talking about going home within the next month to two months, and they've got 11½ months to go. It must be terribly demoralizing for them. Let's see, 41 days is five weeks and six days, isn't it? Oh, honey, I hope that time goes fast. I want to get home so bad.

Our second position was not nearly as good as the first. We were surrounded on all sides by heavy bamboo thickets. Though we were on top of the hill, it would have been no problem for the VC to sneak to within a few feet without being detected. The old sandbagged gun positions of the Aussie 105-mm battery were of little use to us as firing positions. Our 155-mm self-propelled howitzers were too large for them, although we did use some of them for sleeping and ammo bunkers. As for the FDC, laziness got the better of us and we chose one of the sandbagged Aussie firing positions as a common sleeping bunker. We put a sandbagged roof on it and slept the entire off-duty FDC crew in one spot. One well-placed mortar shell would have wiped out half of the crew. We knew better, but for one reason or another we took the easy way out.

Though we didn't shoot much during Portsea, we did fire some interesting missions. The most remembered was in support of ARVN forces near the coast. The mission itself was not that exciting, but the events following made one realize just how long Vietnam had been involved in one war or another. The South Vietnamese troops were moving through a tea plantation one day when they wandered into an unmarked minefield and suffered several casualties. They reported over the radio net that the mines were of Japanese manufacture and probably dated back to the Japanese occupation during World War II. I'd heard of this before, but this was my first personal encounter with it. What a situation—to fight a war in 1967 and still suffer casualties from an enemy long since defeated and gone.

Our FDC took up playing bridge during this operation for lack of anything else to do. Most of the crew, either former college students or college graduates, had played frequently back home, and though some of us were pretty rusty, we forged ahead, learning or relearning as we played. What an odd atmosphere for playing bridge: we sat at our makeshift table concentrating, bidding, with rifles at hand, and every so often jumped up to compute and fire a mission for the Aussies or ARVN. Then, fire mission over, the game resumed. I guess this didn't seem odd to the FDC crew, but having been an FO I could visualize the fear, concern, and discomfort at the other end. To the FO calling for fire, the mission may have been a life or death matter. To us it was just a brief job that had to be done, an interruption of our game.

Midway through Portsea we finally had a little excitement. A female Canadian war correspondent flew in by helicopter and spent several days with us on the hill, conducting interviews, taking photographs, and so on. She spent little if any time with A Battery, as I remember, and seemed interested only in the Aussies, but the presence of a "round-eyed woman" did wonders for morale anyway. The reports we got from the interviewees were interesting to say the least. I don't know if the stories about her nighttime activities were true, but they certainly added spice to her stay. Many an A Battery artilleryman prayed for a personal interview. Though she was not especially attractive in her black slacks, jungle fatigue jacket, and Aussie bush hat, many of our guys would have welcomed any Western woman at this point.

Dearest Frances,                                         5 April 67
What an unthoughtful husband you have. Guess I haven't written in quite a few days now, have I? Operations just aren't conducive to writing, on top of it there's just not much to write. I'm so thankful though that you keep writing as steadily as always. Once we get back to base camp, I suppose you'll get a letter every day or so then. At least I'll try harder then.

Harry has eight more days in country now and Doug nine more. As for myself, 35 days is a bit too long to get too excited.

6 April 67

Today is almost gone. It's about 7:30 P.M., the sun's just down, and it's getting cloudy. The old monsoon rain clouds get heavier every day, and about next month the wet season will be here once again. Hopefully I'll be home before it really sets in.

Doug isn't going home as planned now. His orders changed. He's now going home four days later. Here's the same problem we could have, honey. I might be home as much as five days + or − May 10th. In fact, I could be delayed even more if my replacement doesn't get here on time. So even though we plan on the 10th, it's not beyond the army to change it. Harry, on the other hand, is going home exactly on the date his orders state. So you never know.

Toward the end of the operation we captured a live deer, or I should say I captured it. One morning I was sitting near our mess tent eating breakfast when suddenly there was a loud crashing in the bamboo thicket to my left, a few feet away. My first thought was VC, but before I could even put my food down and grab my rifle, a bush deer broke out of the thicket and ran right in front of me. Hot on his tail and no more than 10 feet behind were a couple of dogs. The dogs took off somewhere after seeing me, but the deer headed for the battery area and ran in among the guns. There was a lot of shouting as some of the gun crew members took off after that little deer. Round and round they ran, with the deer staying within the battery area and all those guys in hot pursuit 20 feet or so behind. I continued to sit there and eat, rather enjoying the whole scene. I could hear them yelling, "Get the deer—fresh venison for dinner!" A chief of section, from one of the howitzer sections, led the pack. Then as I sat there, a spectator to the whole hilarious show, the deer made a sharp turn and headed back my way, retracing his path. I put down my food, and as the deer ran by I nailed him with a flying tackle. What a struggle! Had it not been for the rest of the guys coming up fast and helping, I would have lost him for sure.

We had a deer! The next question was, "Who's going to slit its throat?" They had all been hollering about fresh venison for dinner, but before getting the steaks on the grill there were some preliminaries to perform. It was really kind of funny as those big cannoneers debated who should kill the deer. Finally, at someone's suggestion—maybe mine—they decided fresh venison didn't sound that great after all. So we let the deer up, and it scrambled away and back into the thicket. What irony! Here we were, trained killers really, always anxious to deal Charlie a death blow, and none of us could kill one little deer.

Dearest Frances,                                          12 April 67

In the next couple of days we should be going back to base camp. The operation has just about come to a close, and hopefully, this will be the last one [for me]. I'm pretty sure it is, but you never know. It sure will be good to get back. Then I can start packing and sending things home. Another good thing is that the officers finally have a building to move into. During this operation the few people back at [base] camp put up our tin officers' quarters. So for the first time in almost a year the officers will be out of a tent and off the ground. Actually, the building is comparable to a cattle shed at home, but to us it's wonderful. That's kind of funny, you know. Your dad's hogs and cattle have had better living conditions than I've had this year.

Dear Folks,                                                13 April 67

My writing these days is becoming less and less frequent. I guess it's because it's getting so close to my coming home: 27 more days and I should be on my way.

I am now officially FDO of the btry. Harry Litchfield went home yesterday, and Doug Mistler leaves the 19th. We have a new officer in the btry that will take the FDO job when I leave. I don't think he's going to pan out, though. He's a 1/lt. and couldn't care less about arty. Also, he doesn't know the first thing about it. That's not so bad though; what's bad, he doesn't want to learn. He's a 1/lt. and has been in the army eight years. All he wants is to be put in a maintenance officer slot. So as a result, I think he's trying not to learn his job and thereby get out of it. He doesn't realize, though, that in the meantime he may kill someone because of the lack of effort on his part. I hope we can shape him up.

Apparently now that everyone's about ready to go home, the medals are being dished out. I've been put in for another medal. This is for Operation Junction City. Of course, I must admit an officer has an easier chance of getting medals than a private simply because of the fact that he is an officer. A poor private really has to do something before he gets anything.

On 14 April Operation Portsea ended, and we moved back to Nui Dat. Our return route was the same one we had taken three weeks before and the same I had learned to fear, with good reason, on Operation Ingham. But luck was with us, and we completed the entire trip without encountering one road mine. Something did occur on the way back, however, that I never mentioned to anyone. As we convoyed west on Highway 23 at as high a speed as was possible with our tracked vehicles, we began receiving sniper fire. I was riding up on top of the FDC track when I began to hear (almost feel) pops above my head. I knew from my FO days that we were being shot at, but because of the noise of the vehicle I guess no one else heard the shots. The firing stopped shortly, however, and we rode the rest of the way without further incident.

# 12.THE **F**INAL **D**AYS AND **H**OME AT LAST

Dear Folks,                                                   18 April 67
Say, haven't my letters been getting far and few between lately? I'm afraid it's the result of being so close to coming home. Only 21 more days. I haven't even managed to keep up steady writing to Frances. All the guys are having the same problem, so please bear with me three more weeks.

We've been back from the operation four days now. Everyone's sort of preparing to go home now. The monsoons are starting now too, so we can't leave soon enough.

Darn it, there's just not anything to write. From time to time I'll drop you these little notes. I'll probably stop about the 5th of May. I'll be leaving the btry the 6th if all goes as planned for Long Binh and outprocessing. That's only 17 days away. Time just can't go fast enough now.

My dear sweet wife,                                          24 April 67
Today I got my final orders. I'll be leaving the btry 4 May (10 days) for Long Binh, and at 2:45 P.M. on 9 May (15 days) I board the plane for home. Isn't that great, sweetie? Finally we know almost exactly when I'll be home.

Dear Folks,                                                  26 April 67
Yesterday I received my final departure date from Vietnam. I've got seven days and one hr. left in the btry. On 4 May I leave for Long Binh for outprocessing. My plane leaves from Bien Hoa. Long Binh and Bien Hoa are almost like a suburb to a city; from Long Binh it's just a matter of about a 15 min. drive to the Bien Hoa air base.

So anyway, this long year is almost over now, although like I said once before, it's not really over until you're safely at home or at least on that big silver bird at Bien Hoa. I really can't imagine that this year is almost gone. You just can't imagine how glad I'll be to get back.

Dearest Frances,                                                    28 April 67
    Almost 10 more days now, or 10 days from tomorrow, and I'll be home. Tomorrow night I have to fly to bn HQ (2/35th) for my farewell party, then Thursday I leave the btry, five days from tomorrow. The next five days in Long Binh before I leave for home will be spent processing, in other words doing nothing. So for all practical purposes my tour ends in five days when I leave the btry.
    Of course, I'm working here at base camp. We have fire missions here just like out on operations. For example, today we were shooting for about two hrs. at a VC battalion in our area. In between missions and packing, the officers are building a club. As you know, a large tin building with concrete floor was built for us, so now half of it is being made into a club.

                                                                    2 May 67
    Today the btry went out on another operation. However, because I've only got two days left here after today, I didn't have to go out. I sure felt bad this morning when they all pulled out. I had to say good-bye to everyone. I think at the moment, in particular when I said good-bye to my FDC, the whole year's worth of friendships I've made, frustrations, fears, etc. came to a head. I said good-bye and then as I was walking back to the officers' quarters, it hit me. You know, honey, I actually had tears running down my cheeks. I think a little more and I would have out and out cried like a baby. To think I'll probably never again see these people that I've worked with during the year. You just can't imagine how good friends you make, I guess maybe because we all fear the same things. What really got me was my FDC people saying things like, "We wish you didn't have to leave us, we hope the new officers will be as good," etc. Man, that really tears you up. So honey, even though I want to come home more than anything else in the world, I still hate to leave. I don't know, honey, maybe I'm just getting soft. Believe me, though, it's hard playing the officer fear nothing, hard type for a full year. Someday it will all have to come out, I suppose. When it does, I'll feel like a different person. All

163

these things started building in me since the day I left. After the last tear was shed, the rest of all my emotions during this whole year just have been bottled up. Don't be at all surprised if I cry a little when I meet you seven or eight days from now.

I had mixed emotions about leaving Vietnam. I wanted to go home in the worst way, but I dreaded all the good-byes that had to be said. In addition to A Battery good-byes, there were those to my Aussie and Kiwi mates as well. Saying farewell to the officers of 6RAR would be especially hard. I felt a deep affection for that unit and all the people I had lived and worked with for almost five months. The Kiwis and the Australian Reinforcement Unit, too, held special spots in my heart. Of course not all of the men were around any longer. Some had been killed and others wounded and sent back home. So when I finally said all those good-byes, many of the faces I encountered were new to me: 6RAR and the rest were no longer the same as I had known just a few brief months before.

Even though saying good-bye to everyone was hard and in a sense I hated to leave them all, things were beginning to happen that made me want desperately to get out as soon as possible, for reasons other than just wanting to go home. The Stateside concept of soldiering began catching up with us. First we got rifle racks; then came the order that rifles were to be locked in the racks when not in use. Good grief! We had spent the entire year carrying our weapons wherever we went, even within the base camp area itself, and all of a sudden by an edict from higher headquarters located nowhere near us, we were to keep our weapons locked up. We were still on the perimeter of the Australian Task Force, our base camp had been mortared less than a month before, and several VC regiments still lurked around our area of operation. The war hadn't changed all that much during the year; only our facilities had. But orders were orders, so we installed the rifle racks. We did at least put them in each of the new barracks, where people could get at them. There was also more and more talk about keeping polish on our boots. Our first sergeant even began holding troop formations on one of the battery roads. But topping everything was a call from Vung Tau one day asking if we would play hosts to a couple of helicopter loads of U.S. Army nurses who wanted to come out and see how people lived where the war was. We spent an afternoon in the NCO club making small talk with twenty or so officer-nurses while sipping punch. The whole ridic-ulous affair reminded me of a college sorority and fraternity func-tion. I had hated those artificial gatherings back during my uni-versity days, and I hated this one even more.

The nurses were not the first American women to grace our presence during the year. From time to time we had been visited by the Red Cross "donut dollies." They flew in by helicopter, spent a few hours talking to everyone, and then handed out stationery, pencils, and other morale-building goodies. Actually, the real mo-rale builder for the troops was not the goodies, but the mere sight and perhaps even the touch of an American girl. Then, too, there were all the unspeakable fantasies that accompanied their visits.

Four new officers arrived at A Battery, each destined to replace us "old veterans." I guess we were more than critical enough of them, but except for a few times we never let them or anyone else know of our doubts. We just tried to work them into our jobs as best we could and hoped they would begin to fit in and learn to function before all the old hands, officers and enlisted men alike, left. Two of the four were very promising, but the others seemed to lack any real desire to learn. One, a first lieutenant, seemed more interested in telling us about his sexual adventures than in learn-ing anything. The strangest part was he had photographs to ac-company the stories. He had the rather unusual hobby of taking pictures of himself and his female acquaintances with a time-set 35-mm camera. Of course he had all the pictures with him, and at the drop of a dime he would whip them out and begin yet another description of his love life.

Another officer replacement worried us even more. He knew nothing about artillery, and furthermore he didn't want to learn. By the time I was ready to leave the battery, Chuck, who would be the last of our original officer group to go, was becoming very frustrated. If A Battery was to survive the coming months, the two officers that did seem competent would have to work over-time. I sometimes wish I knew how the new men worked out in the weeks and months following my departure. On the other hand, maybe my memories of the way it was are best.

Dearest Frances,                                    3 May 67
    Today the monsoon finally got under way, I think. Right now our FDC bunker has about an inch of water on the floor. Boy, am I

glad I'm getting out of here. Two more nights and one more day here, and that's it. Then to Long Binh and five days of doing nothing except outprocessing and waiting. Those will be the five slowest days out of the year, I'm sure. Then that big silver bird leaves for home on the afternoon of the 9th.

We had another bad happening yesterday. As I told you, the btry went out on an operation again. They set up in the same place we were on Portsea. Well, two guys stepped on a mine, and one was killed and the other wounded. It just so happens that these same two guys were slightly wounded on Junction City not too long ago. That's the way it goes, though. The wounded guy had his leg amputated yesterday. Today I went to see him at the hospital, and I guess he'll be all right. I took him his wife's picture. He doesn't know yet that his buddy was killed or that his leg is gone. I guess he'll be told in a few days after he gains a little strength. The guy that was killed was single, and the wounded fellow's wife had just had a baby a few days before. I guess if that had to happen, it happened the right way.

Well, darling, time to call it another day. Tomorrow I'll say goodbye to all my Australian infantry friends, and then the next day I'll be in Long Binh. You know, this year seemed to go by fast, but yet just think how far away next May seems. It really has been a long old grind, one that I hope never has to be repeated.

My last full day with A Battery consisted of wandering around and checking my gear into the supply room. As kind of a last Vietnam ceremony, I picked up my final eight malaria tablets to take after I reached home and signed the form stating that I was clear and had received the pills. The last night seemed strange; I had absolutely nothing to do, no responsibilities to fulfill. Nothing! As I went to bed that night I prayed that my sleep would not be interrupted by a mortar attack, a probe on the perimeter, or any other incident smacking of war. I went to sleep worrying that morning might never come.

The next morning I said my final good-byes to the few people left in the battery area and not out on operation, then boarded a jeep for the short trip to the helipad. The wait for the helicopter seemed endless. While sitting there I couldn't help thinking about a story I'd heard of a sergeant who, on his last day, had excitedly tried to board his last helicopter from the rear and had walked into the tail rotor. He was killed instantly. Then, too, I thought of my Kiwi FO colleague who had been killed just eight days before he was due to go home. In Vietnam, I learned, you could take nothing for granted, not even with only hours or minutes left "in country."

The helicopter finally arrived. I boarded very carefully, took a seat, and buckled myself in for the first time in I don't know how many helicopter trips. As we lifted off and began our climb, I looked one last time at Nui Dat, the A Battery position, the 161 Battery area, the rubber trees that held 6RAR, and the more distant rubber plantation battleground north of the village of Long Tan. Then as we flew east around the southern base of the Nui Dinh hills, I settled back in my seat and dreamed of home, hoping the helicopter would make the trip to Long Binh safely.

In no time we landed in Long Binh and I climbed off, elated that my last helicopter ride in Vietnam had been uneventful. A vehicle picked me up at the helipad and took me to the Service Battery area for outprocessing. There were personnel records to complete, pay to get squared away, and orders to post. Most of the time, however, I just lay around and did nothing.

I spent a lot of time sleeping. It was so peaceful without artillery fire. Once I awakened to the sound of Vietnamese women talking somewhere inside the barracks. I had no idea what was going on, but I soon discovered it was Service Battery's housemaids making their rounds, changing sheets, making beds, picking up laundry, and polishing officers' boots. In talking to others I discovered that maid service was common at Long Binh. Vietnamese civilians were used for everything from filling sandbags to serving as maids, and judging from all the barbershops and massage parlors across the highway, for other things as well.

All kinds of thoughts and memories came as I lay on my bunk those last days and hours at Service Battery. Unimportant little things raced through my mind as if I were trying to recall every incident that had happened during the year. I remembered our beer shortage in January, when for some reason American and Australian beer was not available and we had to make do with beer from Korea and Malaya. Boomerang throwing crept into my mind as I recalled the time we first learned to throw them, much to the amusement of our Aussie mates. Thoughts of Armed Forces Radio and TV flashed into focus. One of the biggest jokes of the year for the Aussies had resulted from a slogan Armed Forces TV often used: "Keep up the good work, boys, the folks back home are rooting for you." "Root" was the Australian *F* word. And how could I ever forget the country-and-western music program we listened to every afternoon on Armed Forces Radio, situation permitting. Its theme song, "Buckaroo," ran through my mind again and again as I lay there.

The year in Vietnam had been a memorable one, always characterized by either too much pressure or not enough. When we were busy we were really busy, and when we weren't the boredom was awful. As I recollected all these things, trying to remember what had happened during the year and more than ever thinking ahead to home and the future, I looked at the contents of the old, worn billfold I had carried in a plastic bag the whole time. There were cards I would never need again, military payment certificates that bore no value at all except in Vietnam, and a photo of Frances, now faded, stained with red mud, and almost ruined, but still the best thing, other than letters, that I had to comfort me during these long months.

Dearest Frances,                                                    6 May 67
        Sweetie, I've, or I should say we've, waited for this letter a long time. Yes, this is my last letter to you from Vietnam. You should either get this the day I return or maybe after I've returned by one day. In case of the second possibility, honey, we'll just read this together.

Today I finished my outprocessing. I'll spend tomorrow night again here at Service Btry and then the night of the 8th I'll move to 90th Replacement Bn for final movement to the Bien Hoa air base.

Also today I bought my plane ticket from SF [San Francisco] to Omaha. You can do that here. Then when I get to SF, I'll take the ticket to a window and they'll give me a flight and time, and away I go.

Sweetie, I'm going to close this off. I love you, Frances, and when you get this I'll either be only hours away from home or be there with you already.

All my love darling, Gordon

On the afternoon of 8 May I transferred to the 90th Replacement Battalion for final disposition home. Here all of us from many different units would spend one last night before leaving for home. Most of us were quiet and subdued as we were assigned barracks and bunks.

Next day we all made leisurely final preparations for our departure that afternoon. I put on my khakis for the first time since R&R and then just waited. In the latrine the waste barrels were full of jungle boots and fatigues. A good many GIs were throwing away as much as possible before our final move to Bien Hoa Air Force Base.

The moment of departure for the air base finally arrived, and the excitement began to build. I think everyone was starting to unwind and daring to anticipate what now looked like an almost sure escape, alive, from Vietnam. Arriving at the air base, we stood in line at a couple of places, then finally moved outside under a roof overhang to await our homeward-bound plane. It seemed an awfully long time. Then, like a gift from heaven, our big white jet-liner arrived. Ever so slowly, it approached the loading area. Then it was there, door open and boarding stairway in place. My companions and I stood talking and giggling like children. I could feel the long-awaited finish to this terrible year. Then, as we stood around snapping pictures of one another, the signal to board was given. My time in Vietnam was about to end as we walked those final yards over its concrete-covered soil to our gleaming bird of freedom.

The exhilaration of walking up the steps to the plane defies description. I kept thinking: "I made it, I made it, I'm really going to make it home!" It was wonderful stepping inside and being greeted by the friendly smile of the stewardess as we turned right and walked down the aisle to our seats.

Shortly after we had boarded and settled in, we heard the announcement to fasten our seat belts. A reminder wasn't really necessary; all of us were more than ready. Slowly our plane began to taxi away from the loading point and toward the runway. The engines were given full power, and down the concrete strip we shot. Then the moment came: we were airborne and climbing farther and farther above the land that had been home for almost a year.

If taking off from Vietnam for R&R in February had seemed to take a thousand-pound weight off my shoulders, this seemed to remove a million pounds. What excitement and relief as we climbed away from Bien Hoa! As we flew I stared out the window at the endless shades of green and sometimes brown of the landscape. Here and there you could see the pockmarks of artillery and bomb craters and dead stretches of jungle that had been chemically defoliated. There were the paddies, the streams, and the green rows of rubber plantations. I watched all this as if in a trance, knowing that in all probability I would never see it again. In remember no regret or sadness at all, only happiness and relief. In minutes the coastline and the South China Sea appeared, then Vietnam was behind us and only the blue water lay below. It was over. My tour of duty in Vietnam was truly finished.

As we flew, we kept up a steady stream of conversation. What we said is long forgotten, but I suppose we must have talked about our plans after reaching the United States. It seems strange now that I can't recall any of it. I can remember the smallest details of the trip until the moment we flew over the coastline of Vietnam, but after that the flight is almost a blank. It's as if my brain had operated at peak efficiency for the whole year and then, once the pressure was off, just closed down. For the first time in a year, I must have totally relaxed and let my mind wander, concentrating on nothing in particular except home.

It was daytime on 9 May when we began the final approach to our California landing site, Travis Air Force Base. Though we left Vietnam on the afternoon of the 9th and had flown all night, we gained a day because of time changes and so arrived in the United States on the same day of the month as we left Vietnam. Lower and lower we flew, until finally the gray concrete of the runway flashed past our windows. As the wheels touched down, one of the stewardesses said over the intercom, "Welcome home, boys." What had been a noisy planeload of happy veterans a moment before suddenly became deathly silent. I'm sure all of them, like me, had huge lumps in their throats at that moment. I almost broke down and cried. Then in the next instant, after the stifling silence, everyone cheered.

As we got off the plane, officials guided us into the air terminal. There we emptied our bags and customs people searched through everything with a thoroughness that surprised me. As soon as they finished with us a couple of guys and I hailed a taxi for the trip to San Francisco Airport. The sooner we got there the sooner we might be able to catch a flight home, since we had "space available" tickets. All three of us were going to Denver. We loaded our bags into the taxi and sped off through the freeway traffic. The driver must have sensed our urgency, because in no time we were at the airport.

We paid the cabbie and rushed to the United desk. A flight was just ready to leave for Denver. We ran to the gate but saw a lot of people lined up waiting for boarding passes. The men at the desk began issuing the passes, but as we still stood far back in the line, one of the United employees announced that they wouldn't be able to get everyone on board. My heart sank. How I hated to sit and wait for another flight when we had been so lucky to arrive just in time for this one. Then one of the men asked if anyone in line was just returning from Vietnam. We raised our hands. He motioned us up to the desk and told us he would let us on ahead of the others. I could see some of the civilians were not happy, but I couldn't have cared less. It was good to know that an airline— or at least these particular employees—appreciated our situation and were taking pains to help us. In minutes we were on our way to Denver.

In Denver I was disappointed to find that there was no flight leaving for Omaha until about 10:00 P.M. It meant a fairly long wait, but realistically the timing was perfect. It let me call Frances and tell her exactly when I was getting to Omaha, giving her time to get ready and drive to the airport. Of course I was excited as I dialed home. For the first time since I had called her from Japan during R&R, Frances and I spoke to one another. Considering the moment, we were pretty calm as we hurriedly made final arrangements for our meeting.

The Denver wait passed quickly. I spent the time browsing in the airport gift shops and sipping coffee. All that coffee turned out to be a bad move, however, because the Denver-Omaha flight flew right through a thunderstorm. The lightning flashed, the plane jumped around, and my coffee-laden stomach did flip-flops. The hours I had been airborne, the excitements, the coffee, the countless cigarettes, and now the thunderstorm took their toll. I remember thinking as our plane pitched and rolled over western Nebraska, how ironic it would be if we crashed and I was killed in my own home state after surviving the year in Vietnam. I have to smile thinking about it now, but at that point I prayed in dead earnest, because I was genuinely scared. This was entirely consistent with the past month or so. As I grew "shorter" in Vietnam, I became more and more fearful. I had always reasoned that if I had to die, I wanted to die early in the tour, not after my hopes and my family's were up, anticipating my return.

As we neared Omaha, the weather got better. My stomach even calmed down a little before we landed. Getting off the plane and entering the terminal, I frantically scanned the crowd for Frances. One of my fears while flying home had been for her safety: What if she was killed in an auto accident on the way to Omaha to pick me up? Then I saw her. Just like the movies, we ran toward one another, and the next moment the dream of the whole past year was reality. We were together again. People around us smiled as we embraced. I don't know what we said to one another, but I do remember seeing a family saying good-bye to a soldier. They were all crying.

Being with Frances was finally being home at last. Seeing my parents and sister the next day would also be exciting and emotional, and I could hardly wait, but being reunited with my wife was the ultimate. I could hardly believe I was home, but in the same moment I could hardly imagine I had been gone for almost a year. As we talked, I listened oh so carefully, thinking how different she sounded from what I had remembered. Also, she looked a little different. After a year of trying to remember her face and voice, the image and the real thing didn't quite match. I liked the real thing better. Reaching our car, I loaded my bags, and we drove off to a motel.

The next days were happy ones. The reunion with my parents and sister was especially warm, and I could tell that Dad was very proud of me. I had been among the first from our community, if not the very first, to serve in Vietnam.

During the days we spent with my folks, there was another family gathering. Everyone shook my hand and welcomed me back, and my cousins, some in the National Guard and the Reserves, listened with interest as I talked about Vietnam. We ate a big family dinner, as is typical of our family get-togethers, and played cards during the afternoon as usual. Nothing had changed—only me. Other than what talking I did with my cousins, little was said about Vietnam. One of my aunts, however, capped my homecoming. Echoing her question on my departure, she said, "Well, did you accomplish anything over there?"

# EPILOGUE

I came home from Vietnam believing I'd served my country in a worthwhile cause. I was proud to have done my duty, especially now that it was over, and fully expected the recognition I imagined was due the returning warrior. The boyhood dreams of war heroes and victory marches fairly danced in my head as I returned home. But the old dreams never materialized.

At my family reunion the greeting, "Well, did you accomplish anything over there?" took me aback. That first Sunday at the old home country church I basked in the warm welcome the pastor extended from the pulpit, only to be greeted after church by a member of the congregation who said, "Gordon! How are you? What are you doing with yourself these days?" Later in the week, sitting in my uncle's gas station shooting the bull with friends and a couple of the community patriarchs, I found myself hearing all about the war from them. Still later that week I paid a visit to my old fraternity house on the University of Nebraska campus, hoping to see a few remaining old friends. I don't know what I expected as I walked into the house that day, all decked out in uniform and wearing my new ribbons. I guess I half expected them to jump up, pump my hand, slap me on the back, and break into a fraternity song. Instead there were a few inquiring glances from new faces and the question, "What can I do for you?" I finally did see some of the older brothers, but we mostly made small talk. The big topics of conversation were still girls, final exams, this or that course, and summer rush. It seemed incomprehensible to me that nothing had changed—that while I had been totally caught up in a war, their lives had simply moved along as usual.

In the months and years after returning home I kept track, somewhat, of my battalion, the 2/35th Artillery, as well as the

173

Aussies and New Zealanders. The 2/35th battalion HQ at Xuan Loc was infiltrated by VC sappers some months later, with significant casualties. The battalion as a whole continued its support of operations until March 1971, when it was withdrawn from Vietnam. D Company 6RAR was awarded a U.S. Presidential Unit Citation for the 18 August 1966 battle of Long Tan. Australia and New Zealand increased their troop commitment after I left, with Aussie strength reaching nearly 8,000 and the Kiwis nearly 600 by the end of 1969. By 1971, however, they too withdrew all combat forces, leaving only a few residual New Zealand forces hanging on until 1972 and an Aussie Assistance Group until 1973, when the U.S. commitment in South Vietnam also ended. It was all over.

Leaving the army in 1968 as a captain, I returned to school, earned a master's degree, and have spent the time since as a high-school history teacher. But though the years since Vietnam have been happy, productive ones for me, Frances, and our two sons, the war has never strayed far from my consciousness. In one form or another it still lurks all around as an experience never to be forgotten. Everywhere I turn the reminders leap out at me. From my neighbor down the street whose marine son was killed in Vietnam to my high-school students to whom I teach the history of our involvement in the war, there is no forgetting. From reading books about the war to viewing Hollywood's latest attempt at portraying it, memories remain keen.

Questions about the war from various people over the years, except my history students, have not been many, but they usually are about the same: Were you in the thick of combat? Did you kill anyone? (the question most often asked by students). What about drugs in Vietnam? Were there racial problems? How were the women? The question about the women has always been especially difficult—not giving the answer, but getting anyone to believe it. Time and again I reply that I didn't indulge myself, and time and again I get the same response, that sly, knowing smile that says, "You liar!"

War leaves its mark on the combatant, but in my case it has been only a scratch. Unlike some, I didn't become hateful or cruel. Today I hear some veterans talk about "those dirty dinks," about puncturing bloated bodies and listening to the air escape, about the pleasure of blowing Charlie away, and much, much more. I listen, but I can't relate to that kind of talk. To me the enemy was simply Charlie or the NVA. I feared him and wanted to kill him, but I didn't despise him. To me he was like a dangerous big-game animal to be hunted and killed. Though there were times when I did regard him as human, I remember more clearly the elation of the successful hunt. Despite this, I still don't think of him in hateful or derogatory terms. In fact, I'm ashamed now to think that I ever thought of him as an animal. Perhaps had my total Vietnam experience been worse, I would, as many others do, hold our old enemy in contempt.

Now and again I experience some of the old wartime feelings and sensations. Every so often while hunting along the river I suddenly hear, feel, or sense something that takes me back to the months I spent with the infantry. As I walk among the trees and tangles along the river, it seems at times as if I'm back on patrol with 6RAR. Sounds and smells also bring back memories. The noise of a Huey, for example, sends memories racing through my mind. I suspect that the sound of the helicopter lives on for many a veteran as the symbol of the Vietnam experience. Smells are more difficult to explain, but sometimes in an instant a smell, usually unrecognizable, will send me reeling back to some time and place in Vietnam. I guess those feelings and sensations will never leave me, though they no longer occur as frequently or seem as real as they did during the first years after I came home.

In the early years after my return, I found that many of the things I had enjoyed in the past were no longer pleasurable. For a time I had little desire to read books or watch movies and TV programs dealing with war and killing. I did those things despite myself, but the thrill was gone. As time has passed, however, the enjoyment has returned. Now, as before Vietnam, I like a good war movie and can separate it from what I know about real violence and death.

Some things remain intolerable, however. Invariably, when I show a film or video about war to my high-school history students, one will ask: "Is it in color? Is it bloody?" Even though I know such questions are innocent and ignorant, the thought of a person who knows nothing of real death and violence but wants to see it makes my blood boil. I have had similar feelings at home. When my two sons were young they, like other children, enjoyed playing cowboys, police, and so on. I was uncomfortable when they played these games. Somehow my own sons' pretending to kill each other turned my stomach. That these games were my own favorites as a child seemed to matter little. The thought of killing, even pretend killing, made me remember the real thing too vividly.

I've had small moments of bitterness over the years, but nothing lasting. For example, in 1981, when we finally got the hostages back from Iran, when we heralded their return as heroes and were tying yellow ribbons around all those trees, I wanted to protest. What had they done except get released? What about all the Vietnam War veterans—those who had survived, those who had not, those missing, and all their families? When was the nation going to recognize us? The hostage homecoming, however, seemed to mark a turning point in the American attitude toward Vietnam and everything related to it. In no time the nation did a flip-flop, and all of a sudden we had the Vietnam Memorial, movies, books, and on and on. It reached the point in the late 1980s where my slight bitterness turned to embarrassment, and I began to feel extremely uncomfortable with all the attention the war was being given. Even my history students began to express more interest and ask more questions.

A source of dismay over the years has been the inner conflict between my emotional feelings toward the Vietnam War and my rational ones. It's almost unbearable for me to think that the whole war effort was a waste, that everyone who ever served there did so in vain, but what other conclusion can one reach? In considering the war and all the arguments about why we either should or should not have become involved, the one fact that screams out is that our effort was a failure. Everything we did, every piece of equipment we used, every dollar we spent, every year we served, and every casualty we took was a complete waste. The war, right or wrong, ended for us only after over 50,000 Americans had died, hundreds of thousands had been wounded, some taken prisoner, and many declared missing. For me, like millions of others, a year of my life and of Frances's and my family's was spent apart in the fear and agony of separation for no reason at all. The people I knew who were killed and wounded paid the price for nothing at all. Even though I now am inclined rationally to believe we were incorrect in our foreign policy dealings with the South Vietnamese, viewing the whole affair the way many of our experts saw the

China situation shortly before Mao's takeover in 1949, I still cannot stomach the thought of our giving up and leaving the war as we did. Some, of course, would argue that we didn't give up. In a completely military sense I agree, partially. But our nation did capitulate psychologically. So even though on a purely rational basis I might conclude now that we never should have gotten involved as we did in Southeast Asia, my emotions tell me that we could and should have pressed the whole stinking mess to a military conclusion in our favor. What a feeling it is to know you've served your country and offered your life for absolutely nothing in the end. Yet I'm one of the lucky ones! What of all the families missing loved ones or all those still enduring the pain of losing parts of their bodies or still suffering the emotional scars of combat?

Why was I one of the lucky ones? This haunts me from time to time. Given a little different timing, I could just as well have been with D Company 6RAR on 18 August 1966. Given a little different setting in direction or elevation, one of the mortar rounds taken in base camp or the fire support base could have wounded or killed me. Given a different position in our convoys on Operation Ingham or Junction City, I could have been blown up by a mine. Given a different time, place, or unit assignment, I could have been involved in heavier or more continuous fighting, my battery could have been overrun, and so on. Given changes in any of the many variables, my tour of duty could have been far different from the rather mild combat experience it was. Why was my C Company 6RAR Aussie lieutenant friend spared death in Vietnam only to catch malaria, be shipped home, and then die in a traffic accident? Why was my Kiwi FO colleague, who had already spent almost 18 months in Vietnam, who was married and the father of three children, killed just days before leaving for home? Why do things work out as they do? Is it luck, God's will, or what? From a human standpoint it seems a mystery, but biblically the issue clears: "In all things God works for the good of those who love him, who have been called according to his purpose" (Rom. 8:28). Perhaps the mystery is really a challenge for those who survived to seek and fulfill that purpose.

It's hard to believe now that so many years have gone by since the Vietnam War, or to comprehend that one year out of my life could leave memories beyond nearly anything else I ever experienced. As we blunder through life, many things seem "the most important" to us from time to time, whether it's the big game of the season, high-school or college graduation, marriage, the birth of our children, or some current tragedy. The experience of war, however, may very well rise above it all. For many of us who survived and care to remember, war may have been the one great adventure of a lifetime, never to be equaled. For some, everything else in life may pale by comparison. For me, the Vietnam War remains a composite of bad and good memories, the most treasured of which are my recollections of A Battery and of our Australian and New Zealand allies and mates.

# INDEX

**M**ap 1

Phuoc Tuy Province

Laos

*Operation Ingham*

Nui Dinh Hills

*Operation Vaucluse*

Nui Dat

Long Tan

*Operation Portsea*

Baria

*Operation Smithfield*

Vung Tau

0        10        20 miles

Qui Nhon

South Vietnam

Cambodia

Nha Tr

Cam Ra

*Iron Triangle (War Zone D)*

Bien Hoa

Xuan Loc

Saigon

0        50        100 mi